Chronicles

Of

Lincoln County

Tales of ghost towns, trails
And
Other Haunting Tales

John LaBorde

ISBN: 1495365980
ISBN-13:9781495365980

CONTENTS

Ghost Riders
Hall Station, Sanborn, Kutch and Pierces
McColin
Girard
Kendrick
Cowan's
Forder
Hollywood
The Spirits of Clifford
Haunted Farms - Genoa

1 County roads lead to forgotten places

Back Roads

The trail wound along by the sand crick, curling to and fro as the water washed the sand away from the banks. Here and there the ruts of the pioneer wagon wheels could be seen. The Indians had followed this trace for years chasing the buffalo. Today these ruts are gone and mostly forgotten. Roads now follow the lines of the surveyors, sliding up and down the hills, crossing the cricks, bending around tricky parts and correction line curves.

Off the buzzing freeway, here are the sounds of the prairie. There are ponds where wildlife abounds, shaded groves of tall trees, Barns standing stately over the plains, a lone tree, with a foundation where there was once a homestead, the country church on the ridge and nearby is the country school.

Driving the roads of back country takes one to places where dreams were lived and lost, where dreamers found theirs and memories abound.

Many a community barn no longer stands. Talk with a local and they will tell you about the dances there, the card parties, weddings and other celebrations. They will let one know what happened to the barn, most were torn down because of neglect. Take a moment, step back in time. Here on the corner of the road intersection stands a few trees, a foundation peeks out o the dirt, old wind mill still stands next to the water tank. Across the way is more relics of foundations, steps, walls and a ways down the road is a church.

Many settlers would build their homes near other settlers and a community would build. Many of these people shared a common background or families. They would have similar traditions and celebrations. Sometimes this little collection of homes would have a Post Office and nearby was the school. These moments in the past are gone, only memories or stories from a few old timers.

2 Relics from days past mark many a driveway

The wagon creaked as it climbed up the ridge, horses straining to pull the wagon upwards. Out there in the pasture can be seen the ruts of old wagon trails.

Today the dust boils off the pick up truck as it hustles down the road. Years ago it may have been on its way to the still to pick up some mason jars for the dance that weekend.

Over there is a collapsed shed, pens barely visible along the side, and over there is the potato patch. The pigs dined real good after the mash was cooked off. For years the farm was a focus of a few. Here was the country purveyor of fine made home brew. Most neighbors never knew what was going on under the pig shed.

This was one of many stills that dotted the prairie during the early 1900's. Come Sat. eve one of the locals would be at the community barn dance with a pick up, back covered by a tarp. During intermissions he was a busy person.

The community barn hosted many an activity, town was a day's ride away for many a settler. Over there a half hours ride was the barn. Hook the buggy up and go visiting, play cards, work on quilts and let the children play. This was the neighborhood of the pioneer.

3 Trees and a windmill tower mark where a home had once stood

During the high heat of summer the prairie animals seek out shade for cool. The arc of the sun declines to the far horizon. Cool of the evening approaches, animals stir from the shade, seek out some water. On far hillside can be seen the antelope watching the travelers below. High overhead circles the hawk, riding the thermals. Coyote trots along the fence line searching, turkeys pecking away at the gravel and the birds sing with the sun's passing. Here one sees and hears a life that has no peer. High mountain peaks on the horizon set a backdrop for the drama that unfolds at its feet.

Pikes Peak shades the setting sun, the breeze sets down and a quiet beyond description envelopes the grassland. Dusk slides over the land, the natives get ready for a nights rest. A soft chirping whispers as the birds talk for a last moment. The hoot of the owl says he is ready to go hunting, Wail of the coyote shatters the evening calm, their convention of yips and barks penetrate through the howl. Soon they move on and the flutter of the night hawks wings ruffle overhead. Be still and listen for it is only on the prairie.

The golden shade of the cotton woods glow across the plains. A yellow ribbon marks the line of the sand crick. Arched tree limbs invite a moment of brief respite.

Small ponds dot the land. Birds flock to them. Ducks swim around searching for food, the occasional Great Blue Herron lights on the ponds shore to fish, deer cautiously approach.

Country roads, winding, dusty, over hill and traveling across the land. Over there on the rise is a grove of trees, out back was the shed over a cellar that held the still. Through the night it would cook, in the morning mason jars were filled and carried to the barn. Later that week a panel wagon would drive up and back into the barn at night. The clank of jars could be heard as it was loaded.

Next day it would drive off to the neighboring villages making deliveries. On Saturday a model T pick up would pull in the farm yard. A bit later the driver would walk out of the house and get into his pick up and drive over to the barn. Backing in through the opened doors he would hop out and walk back to help the farmer load his pickup. Tarp was tied over the load and out onto the road he would drive.

Lincoln County

That evening he could be seen at the barn on the other side of the county. The faint plucking of the guitar and the fiddle could be heard along with the crooner and toe tapping inside the community barn. Shadows lengthened as a sliver of moon came over the hill. Out the barn door a couple walks, hand in hand, out to the parking. Opening the door she climbs in, he whispers a few things and closes the car door. He walks over to the pickup, nods his head, pleasantries are exchanged and in whispers a conversation ensues.

Corn cob pipe is glowing in the dim moonlight, the young man reaches into his pocket, draws out some coins, counts them out and hands em to the guy with the pipe. Under the tarp his arm dives, a slight tinkle of glass can be heard. A small jar slides out from under the covering. Handing it to the young man, there is nodding, a smile surrounds the pipe as the young man walks off.

4 Machines rusting away, line empty property now abandoned

Soon a car door slams, light glimmers as cigarettes are lit, there is giggling as the mason container is raised to lips. Quietness sets over the evening.

Country roads, curving, winding, rolling over hills, traveling across the land. Over there among the twisted trees was the homestead. Here grandpa and grandma began their dreams. They worked the land, raised a family, built a home, survived the dust storms, out lasted the winter blizzards.

No longer are the buildings there. The tornado came through, ripped the barn apart, flattened the chicken coop, tore the shop and granary to shreds and spread the pieces into the neighbors' fields. A depression is left where the house had set over the cellar. Dreams and memories twisted to shreds like the battered trees, pieces flying in the wind.

Yellow school bus rumbles past, going to a school that has disappeared, heading into a town that is no longer.

Ghosts ride the bar ditches of times past. Towns float in memory pockets. Stories are waiting ears to listen. Wind silently glides past.

Country roads, winding, curving, rolling over hills and traveling across the land. A farm pond glistens in the late afternoon sun. Fish making circles to float on the sheen, ducks rest on the water, waiting the icy fingers of the north to push them on south. Yellow leaves shine in the light waving good bye to summer. The land is settling down for the winter. White blanket covers the prairie, animals hunker down looking for warmth. Sun passes over head warming the land.

A drive on the country roads leads to many wonders for those who seek them out. Past ranches, cattle grazing nearby, plowed fields of the farmers, equipment parked by the fields waiting guiding hands. Windmills twirl drawing the ribbon of life out of the ground, nourishing life on the grasses. Life is lived out on the prairie at its pace.

The Kay-Pee

Across the high plains of eastern Colorado rolls the rails of the Union Pacific Railroad. It is not a busy line, the occasional coal train, grain hoppers and mixed freight pound the rails that were first laid in 1870. It is the first railroad that had Colorado as its destination. In the NE corner of the state the Union Pacific cut the corner at Julesburg on its way west. The railroad over the central plains of Colorado to the south of the UP had its beginning as a rival to the Union Pacific to the north. Both wanted to reach the west coast and both started on the Missouri River.

In 1862 Congress passed the Pacific Railway Act. This gave alternating sections of land for railway construction and it also provided bonding of $16,000.00 per mile for construction. With this money dangling like a carrot, there were numerous companies that sprung up wanting to chase the government dollar to the Pacific Ocean.

The Leavenworth, Pawnee and Western RR was a shell corporation from 1855. A group of investors acquired this company and reorganized it, renaming it the Union Pacific Eastern Division. This group of investors was well connected, one was an eastern banker and the other had military and political connections. With these connections, financicring was obtained with some government help. Westward from Wyandotte, Kansas, the railroad began construction

5 A Union Pacific passenger special rolls across the prairie

6 Executives of the Union Pacific tour the KP line

To the north the Union Pacific railroad was organized and they were building west from Omaha, Nebraska. The race was on, both were well financed and making good progress. The Union Pacific became embroiled in some shenanigans and had a few problems. To the south the Union Pacific Eastern Division was being associated with the skull drudgery. They dropped the name Union Pacific and became the Kansas Pacific. To this day this section of railroad is still referred to as the Kansas Pacific.

With the name change the fledgling railroad gained some impetus, more financing was secured and construction was moving along at a good clip. Their progress was ahead of their rival to the north. Plans were made to build the railroad along the Republican River into Nebraska and then follow the Overland Trail to the Pacific. This is the route the Union Pacific was going to follow but they were floundering in so much scandal, construction was stalled and the Kansas Pacific was out front.

The glory of the Kansas pacific, KP, would soon fade for the principal players got into a power struggle. One of the parties was ousted and this upset many of his followers. On an inspection trip the new boss was confronted by a friend of the ousted principal. The disgruntled employee took serious umbrage with the new boss and after some heated words the man pulled out a gun and shot the boss.

This death put a huge roadblock in the construction of the rails. The brother of the deposed boss did not have the abilities of his brother and suddenly what had been a smooth operation ground to a halt in corporate turmoil. This upheaval in the KP gave the UP time to get back together and regain the lead.

~~~~~~~~~~~~~~~~~

Losing their advantage the KP had to rethink their strategy. No longer was the Republican River a viable route. Gold had been discovered in the Rocky Mountains and a new city of Denver was growing. Reaching the gold fields and Denver became the focus of the new corporate group of the KP. The most direct route to the mountains was the Smoky Hill Trail. At the river junctions, the Republican route was dropped in favor of following the Smoky Hill River across western Kansas to Colorado and the new gold rush.

Here on the Smoky Hill Trail was a fairly easy route for the railroad to follow. The trail had been mapped by the military and there were stage routes going west to Denver. The stage line had laid out where the springs for water were. Utilizing this information the railway could easily plot out their route only making variations to keep the Right of Way grade as easy as possible.

7 One of many coal trains retuns to the coal mines to be reloaded

Westward the Kansas Pacific continued building. On the political horizon, civil discontent was brewing. Soon the War Between the States would break out. This Civil War made it difficult for the railroad to obtain construction funds, with all the money being diverted into the war effort.

The railway had made it as far west as Ft Sheridan, Wallace Kansas, in 1868. Here the construction stalled out. For over a year, this was the end of the rails. With the conclusion of the Civil War, funds became available again.

Westward construction resumed again in the fall of 1869. A General William Palmer was hired as their construction manager. A new found vigor was found and the pace of construction dramatically picked up. From this spot in Kansas to Denver it took less then a year to complete. More roadway was built and track was laid in this time then the previous seven years. This new found energy was not without its problems.

~~~~~~~~~~~~~~~~~~

The fledgling railroad had been beset with Indian attacks all across Kansas and entering Colorado the attacks did not stop. Then there the massive buffalo herds, temporarily halting construction at times. These problems continued to plague the railway.

Progress continued on the new railroad. The rail head had reached Kit Carson, Colorado and General Palmer had moved his headquarters there. At the time Kit Carson was boasting a population of around 5000 souls. The work gangs of the railroad would number about 100 workers and they were stretched as far west as Lake Station, a stage stop.

Along this route were bridge and grading crews preparing the right of way for the laying of ties then the iron rails. At Lake Station the survey crew was set up and the chief engineer was getting ready to survey more of the route westward.

The spring of 1870 the Cheyenne Indians launched a series of coordinated raids on the railroad work crews and stage stations from Kit Carson to Lake Station. The raiding parties were small, 10 to 15 Indians, yet there were a number of work crews out that were attacked plus the stage stations. It is estimated that about 200 Indians took part in the raids. The chief engineer at Lake Station was killed, along with other workers. Others were seriously wounded and all were scared. Back to the Kit Carson the railroad workers fled to the protection there.

General Palmer did not like having his workers scared and afraid to work out in the prairie to the west. The General got on the singing wire and telegraphed Washington DC wanting protection. General William Custer had been reinstated to his command and his calvary troops were assigned to protect the Kansas Pacific Railroad as they built westward. The Calvary patrolled the KP from Kit Carson into Denver.

After Custer arrived most of the Indian raids stopped. The Cheyenne Indians had traveled north to meet up with the Sioux and at a later date meet Custer on the Little Big Horn River. The Arapahoe Indians had gone south to the Indian Territory in Oklahoma. Still Custer remained on assignment to patrol the KP for six months.

~~~~~~~~~~~~~~~~~~

The other problem the railway had was with suppliers. The place that had been shipping ties from eastern Kansas had stopped and they could not find another place back there to supply them with rail ties. William Palmer went to Denver and got the interest of the bullwhackers that had been hauling supplies into the gold mines. Most were returning back east or to Mexico empty. General Palmer made them an offer that got them to hauling ties out for his railroad. There were sawmills in the Elbert, Pinery and other places that would supply the railroad with ties. Over 800 teams of oxen and 700 teams of mules were hauling ties to the railroad.

Buffalo hunters had been hired to provide meat for the workers and as such much of the buffalo problem was alleviated. One such hunter the railway hired was a German Baron, James Walk. He would travel to the prairie with his hunting party and supplying the railroad with fresh buffalo meat. The Baron went to the area north Limon close to the head waters of the Arickaree River for his hunting camp. Here there was a spring and the river had a good flow of water. The buffalo were plentiful and life was good for the hunters.

This buffalo camp still exists today and is called Walks Camp. After the Baron left, the settlers that had moved in the area stared using the camp for picnics and meetings. It became like a community park owned by the locals and is still owned today by some of their ancestors, those odd quirks from the early days of railroading.

━━━━━━━━━━━━━━━━━

With the major problems under control or gone the rails continued to be laid. July of 1870 the rail head had reached present day town of Hugo. Here was the mid way point between Sharon Springs, Kansas and Denver, Colorado. The new town of Hugo was designated a division point and a roundhouse was built, near where the swimming pool is now located. Other structures were added and Hugo was becoming a major railroad town.

While the KP was being built across Colorado another group had formed the Denver Pacific Railway Company to build a railroad from Cheyenne, Wyoming to Denver, Colorado. These two companies had held discussions for when they get to Denver. During these discussions the Denver Pacific had financial difficulties and John Evans, one of the principals of the Denver Pacific worked out an agreement with the KP. The KP was to supply the necessary support for the DP to finish their line to Denver. In return the KP got controlling interest in the DP. A couple of years later the KP acquired the DP.

With this backing, the DP finished their line into Denver at about the same time the KP got to Hugo. The two railroads agreed to jointly operate the line from Hugo to Denver. The DP crews would start building from Denver eastward and the KP from Hugo westward. Strasburg was the midway point and the race was on between the two crews to see who would reach this point first.

When these two crews finished the first transcontinental railroad would be complete. For the KP had a bridge over the Missouri River and the UP didn't. For many it is a splitting of hairs but one could travel coast to coast now on the railroad without getting off the train and taking a ferry across the river. The Silver Spike monument sits in small park in Strasburg, somewhat forgotten and languishes in the shadows of the giant railroad to the north.

~~~~~~~~~~~~~~~

The railroad was not exempt from train robberies, just that most were not reported. The railroads did not want public knowledge of what they were carrying and of robberies in fear that others would rob their trains. The railroad had their own police and used people like Pinkerton to work on their robberies. The local sheriff could not do things like their own police did.

There is the story of the train robbery that took place in the late 1800's. The robbers jumped on the train near Limon and went through the train helping themselves to the passengers valuables. Just before arriving at Hugo the bandits jumped off the train and disappeared into the frontier. By the time the train arrived in Hugo the bandits had a great head start on the marshal and his posse. Robbing a train in the middle of somewhere gave the crooks a jump on the law and could easily disappear.

Then there was the gang headquartered in Kit Carson, CO. Apparently it was well organized, from stories, the gang involved some railroad police and local constables. The gang had the reputation for roaming far and wide, with the ability to make a train disappear.

The railroad had brought a variety of people to the open prairie of eastern Colorado and a few found some good picken's of other people stuff. The payroll train would travel the rails west on a regular basis to pay the workers. There were no reports of it being robbed but it would have made a nice target.

8 The 844 steam engine travels across the KP on its way home to Cheyenne, WY

With the completion of the rails into Denver the trails shifted to follow along next to the tracks. There was a certain amount of security for people traveling by wagon to be near the rails. There were now settlements at the various railroad stops. Here water and supplies could be had as well as help for breakdowns.

Driving the wagon west the oxen would be put out to pasture at night and the next morning the oxen would be rounded up and put back in yoke to continue the pull west. One such traveler was doing that but one morning didn't have success in finding his oxen. For three days he searched the surrounding prairie looking for his cattle. Finally he gave up, went to the nearby town, took the train to Denver and bought two yoke of ox.

He drove them back to where his wagon and family were parked. That evening he released the oxen to graze. Next morning he got on his horse, rode out looking. No oxen were to be found. He got somebody in another wagon to let him hitch onto their wagon and for $200.00 he got his wagon towed into Denver.

First response of many, it was Indians. Maybe but that gang in Kit Carson probably had a good market for oxen. At $100.00 a yoke, oxen were pretty profitable.

~~~~~~~~~~

In 1872 the KP bought the DP and one year later the KP was in receivership. During this time, the big financial moguls in New York were investing in various railroads. Jay Gould was buying stock in the KP and the UP. Gould bought enough stock in the KP that he gained controlling interest in the railroad. Gould was also influential in the circles of the Union Pacific RR.

During this time Jay Gould did some wheeling and dealing with his railroad holdings. With some pressure, one report said, blackmail, Gould got the UP to absorb the KP into its system. In 1880 the KP was no longer, it was now a part of the Union Pacific RR. Off of this transaction Jay Gould's railroad stock went over the top and the "Robber Baron" made millions off of a railroad that had been in receivership just a few years earlier.

~~~~~~~~~~

The railroad across the frontier changed many things. No longer was the journey westward a trip of weeks. Now one could catch the train and be west in a few days. Supplies from the east traveled by rail and arrived promptly. Mail service was by train now. All this opened up the frontier along the rails. Settlers moved west, settling on the land, communities were built and shops were opened. The settler could now go to the big city in a short trip, or go to the county seat and back in a day. They could ride into town, leave their horse at the livery stable, catch the train and be back that evening. Pick up their horse and go home. Many of the epic trips for the early pioneer were over.

~~~~~~~~~~~~

Today the UP still operates a few trains on the old Kansas Pacific line. The right of way that was laid in the 1860's and finished in 1870 hasn't changed much. A few curves were straightened out, otherwise it is the same roadbed, more than 140 years old. US Hwy 40 followed the railroad ROW for years and the highway department straightened out their highway, they left behind some remnants of the old roadway. On this old section one can travel along next to the rails like the early pioneers did.

It runs from the ghost town of Clifford to the ghost town of Aroya. Many of the old buildings are gone. Here there were stage stations, Indian battles and roaming buffalo. The little towns that the highway went off and left are pretty much gone. The winds of time whistle among the ruins of the buildings the railroad helped to build. Take a step back in time along the *Golden Belt Route.*

9   Oil rigs now dot the land, searching out deep in the ground

Golden Belt Route

Just south of US Highway 40/287 junction with State Highway 94 is a remnant of the old Golden Belt Route. When the government changed the ROW of US 40 they left behind the old highway for ranch access. Just before the railroad crossing is a dusty country road that appears to go nowhere. Yet this country road takes one back in time, a living museum.

Traveling west, just across the county line a short distance is the Aroya stage stop from the 1860's Looking south over the railroad tracks in a ranchers pasture is roughly where the stage station had been located. There are no marking's left and the stone marker from the stage operator is probably a souvenir somewhere.

Pause on the rise and listen. In the distance can be heard the cry of the stage driver, urging his team onwards. Hoof beats pounding the trail. Ahead the station master is doing some last minute checking of the harness on the fresh set of horses. Soon the lathered horses will gallop into the station, unhitched and a fresh set latched onto the stage. At a full gallop the stage with fresh horses will charge out of the station onto the next stop at Boyero. Many a story has grown in the area of these ghost stages rolling across the plains, Indians in hot pursuit. Stagecoach making it into the station, gate fling closed, passengers jumping out with rifles, firing at the Indians. Shortly it is quiet as the Indians retreat into the woods of the sand creek. Hollywood did not have to write a script for these were actual events along the route.

The Golden Belt Route was the shortest distance between St Louis and Denver. When the Interstate was built some politicians got the routing to be designated along the Interstate. Yet here along this short piece of country road one can see how the early travelers traveled. A museum could not recreate this short route that was left behind. There is a couple of old concrete bridges on the route from when the government road builders thought concrete was their solution to road construction.

10 One of the early bridges is slowly crumbling. Built for early day travels on the higway by the rails.

At the turn of the century wagons were still plying this road and when the horseless carriage was built they used the wagon roads. Look ahead as the wagon rolls over the prairie. Small puffs of dust rolling off the oxen, dust boiling up from the wheels, the settlers stoically walk beside the wagon. High sun overhead, the heat shimmers over the grasslands. Children walk beside their parents, staying in the shade of the covered Prairie Schooner. Up to the wagon, dad strides, lifting a tin cup off a hook, he raises the lid on the water barrel and dips out a cup of water. Not breaking stride, dad walks along drinking the water.

Off in the distance can be heard a sputtering. A cloud of dust appears behind them and is growing closer. Shortly it goes beep beep and passes them. The tin lizzie wades through the wagon ruts bouncing to and fro. The driver waves as the roll by. Soon its cloud of dust is no longer visible on the horizon. The settlers in their wagon continue their trod on westward to their destination.

Here time hasn't changed the prairie much. A keen eye may spy the Bald Eagles resting in the trees down by the sand creek. There is the ambassador of the plains, the Western Meadow Lark. His distinctive chirp greets the traveler. The small birds scurry along the grasses searching out bugs. Overhead floats the Prairie Flacon or maybe a circling hawk. The Colorado prairie has one of the largest varieties of birds in the state. There is the Rocky Mountain Plover that passes through in the spring that gets mistaken for a Killdeer.

In the woods of the Big Sandy lounge the deer in the

shade of the giant cottonwoods. Nearby are pools of water and lush grass on the banks. Out on the hillside are the watchers, Antelope. As one travels along the road they keep a sharp eye on the visitors. There are a variety of herds in the area and most like a good distance from strangers.

Here is a land that hasn't changed much from when the first gold seekers stumbled across Colorado to the Rocky Mountain gold fields. When the highway was moved lots of the original character was kept. In the summer of 1870 the railroad pushed its iron rails across the prairie. The Smoky Hill Trail moved to follow along beside and the stagecoach faded into pages of history and the Indians had been chased north or to Oklahoma. The Golden Belt Route had become a high speed conveyance. The train had reduced the time from back east to the mountains and the Smoky Hill trail was now easy to follow.

11 A catalogue home still stands by the railroad.

In the 1850's when the trail was first laid out many a traveler got lost traveling west. Large mounds of dirt were used to spot the trail. Only the buffaloes thought these dirt piles were a great place to wallow. Then the big rush hit. One Denver newspaper estimates that over 100,000 travelers passed through Denver, that summer on their way to the gold fields.

The route along through here would have been congested. People headed for the Colorado in many a manner. Pictures show them pushing wheelbarrows, pulling a hand cart, leading a burro or just walking carrying a knapsack. Gold is a driving fever and all shapes and sizes of the fever passed through this area.

Today this little country road is quiet. Maybe meet one or two vehicles, possibly a long coal train may pass by. Ahead lays the ghosts of Boyero, a little community that refuses to roll up main street.

12 The country school, a silent reminder of other days.

Boyero

South of US 40/287 a few miles is the ghostly collection of Boyero. There are still a few residents of Boyero and they have their own Post Office. One of the old buildings was made into an antique store and the occasional traveler will turn off the highway. If the proprietor is around there is a treat awaiting the visitor, for there are stories galore for the patient ear. If not..... oh well, enjoy the sights.

13 Few of the old buildings still stand.

Boyero got its beginning as a stage stop on the Golden Belt Route. Here there is good water for the stage line. The Smoky Hill Trail passed through the area and was followed by the railroad. It is from the railroad that the community got its growth.

Boyero was a major stop for maintenance workers on the railroad. Up and down the rails these workers moved keeping the rails in tip top shape. It also became a prime ranch area and it is ranching that keeps the community going.

The original streets the railroad platted out are still visible and many of the foundations are still visible along these now abandoned streets. The old general store finally gave up and is now but a concrete slab where it once stood. There are a few smaller buildings standing in various state of decay or care. Across the way is the building of mystery.

A large two story building looks at the tracks, it has a building added to it. Myths and lore of other days abound from its roof top. Was it a boarding house, the mansion for the local big boss or maybe the quarters for the rough and tumble rancher? Did the local gang of outlaws stop in here? Was it place for the drummers to stay, what kind of big deals were made. Did the railroad house their traveling workers here? Stop by some evening and witness the clatter and clanking as the lantern is set on the table. Footsteps across the front porch, chairs rattle as they are moved up to the table. Matches flicker as pipes and cigars are lit. The sound of cards shuffling echoes across the eve and banter begins.

Boyero was also a stop along the Texas/Montana cattle trail. There are numerous ponds in the area and the store had good stores for the herd.

The tinkle of the saloon piano is silent. No longer do the high booted cowboys roll into town for a weekend celebration.

The old Golden Belt Route provides a look back in to another time.

Clifford

Traveling along the old Golden Belt route one runs out of old road. The Lady Bird Memorial rest area marks the end of the old dusty road. Here CR 39 joins the re-routed US Hwy 40/287.

Just a short distance south of this junction is where the community of Clifford had been. The one room school house is still there. It sits in a ranchers pasture, private property, and he occasionally puts his bulls in there during the off season. The bulls like to lounge in the shade on the tiny school house.

14 Union Pacific engineering special passes through Clifford.

If one pauses nearby they may catch the school marm hustling out to the shed in back, coal bucket in tow. Maybe it's recess time and the dozen or so children are out playing. Maybe they are on the merry go round or on the swings. The gleeful laugh of little children fills the air of the prairie.

No longer are the streets of Clifford visible. Nature has reclaimed them. Near the railroad tracks is a grove of giant cottonwood trees. Stretched along the rails are bits of foundations and footers from the structures that stood next to the rails.

15 Footers of buildings and other structures are all that remain of Clifford next to the rails.

In the distance can be heard the whistle of the train as smoke rises up into the sky. It is the pay train and the depot is busy in anticipation of pay day. The tiny railroad town thrives on the money this train brings.

South of the tracks, behind gated fence with no

trespassing signs is the classic haunted house. Rising into the air to caress the tree tops is a Montgomery Ward catalogue house. Was it a rooming house or the home of the local rancher baron? Weather and neglect have taken its toll on the classic old house. The porches have collapsed, windows gone and parts of the roof missing.

Be out here in the evening when the meal is being served. Kerosene lanterns flicker on the dining room table that is full, voices echo out the windows. Conversation is fast and furious about the day's happenings. The myths of the house abound. Lights flash in the windows, the amber glow of a pipe on the porch and shadows float around the corner. There are as many stories about the house as there were pages in a Montgomery Ward catalogue.

Near by is Mirage, the stage station. There are no traces of the station left. Here is a spring n stream pushing the Smoky Hill Trail a bit north, until a bridge was built over the stream. Today the bridge is concrete from the early 1900's, a testimony to the durability of the bridge construction.

In the woods the Indians would wait for the stage and launch attacks. Later out of these woods the Indians would charge the railroad workers. This was the home of the Indians. Along this waterway they would follow the buffalo that grazed nearby on the grasses of the prairie.

With a short drive down a forgotten dusty road, one can visit a piece of history that even Hollywood could not script. Early gold seekers, wagon trains, stage coaches and railroad construction into the heart of Indian territory. Monster cattle drives across the prairie, raging grass fires, it all happened.

Hugo

Just to the west of present day Hugo the Big Sandy Crick makes a sweeping curve. In this area is where the Leavenworth and Pikes Peak stage and freight line is suspected to have built a stage station. The L&PP did not follow the Smoky Hill Trail, they surveyed their own route to the Rocky Mountain gold fields.

Figure 16 The Roundhouse sits in silence, a reminder of other days.

Here in this flat area are small pools of live water and good grass, making it an ideal spot for a stop. Being on private property, there has not been a close survey of the site to confirm. Yet in this area one can watch the teamsters as the wagon trains from Leavenworth roll in for the night.

Sitting on the ridge to the east one can look down on the area and see the campfires of the early day freighters. Nearby their oxen and mules graze on the grass, the water holes are busy. These wagon trains were 40 to 60 wagons long and bigger. Soon there will be activity for the stage is approaching. The station master has prepared a new hitch of horses. Into the station the stagecoach gallops and there is a frenzy of activity as the horses are changed out. As the horses gallop off the teamsters settle back down around the fires and share more tall tales of their trips across Indian land.

Here at Hugo the Leavenworth and Pikes Peak trail crossed the Smoky Hill Trail. From Hugo westward the freight line followed parts of the Smoky Hill Trail. To the north of town there are still some ruts visible from the trails.

17 A UP train passes by the Cap Barron spring.

The Leavenworth and Pikes Peak Line was short lived. Just over two years after it began, it closed up shop. The road was abandoned and silence sat on the prairie. For the discerning ear though, one can still hear the crack of the whip as the drivers urged their teams over the hills and westward. Down the hill into the lush basin by the Big Sandy the wagons rolled to a stop.

When the Leavenworth and Pikes Peak closed down the Butterfield Overland Dispatch started a stage route to the gold fields of the Rocky Mountains. The BOD for the most part trailed along the Smoky Hill Trail, going from the Railhead in Kansas across Colorado to Denver.

The BOD built their station Willow Springs just east of Hugo on Willow Creek. Here there was a spring and some small pools. The Lincoln County Fairgrounds are a part of the station. To the north of the fairgrounds went the Smokey Hill trail and the east edge is believed to be where the stage station was.

Being built of adobe and sod there was seldom much left to track where the stop was. The rock markers quite often were collected by souvenir hunters. Yet this is all visible from Highway 40/287. It is a horse pasture today and gives an old time feeling of when the stage stopped here.

Among the trees of Hugo today there are a plethora of ghosts. There is the roundhouse, Hedlund House, the WPA structures, Town Hall and the swimming pool, and there is the depot.

The street that goes to the roundhouse dates from the 1800's. This is the area where the railroad built section houses and various railroad related structures. Take a stroll around the roundhouse, it was built in 1909. Listen to the clang and pounding of metal work from within. Hear the chuffing of the steam engine that sits on the turn table. Nearby are the footers for the other buildings. The wail of the whistle rolls across the valley as fast freight approaches from the west. Soon it will stop at the depot and will be serviced. Next is the crack passenger train from St Louis to Portland.

Passengers and drayage are unloaded and loaded at the depot. The engine is uncoupled and rolls away to the roundhouse as another engine waits nearby to hook on to the train to continue the journey. It is a picture from a bygone era. Today the roundhouse sits in silent testimony to those past days.

The depot was moved a number of years ago and a park was built around it. There is a playground and picnic tables. One can pause for a moment and listen to the wig wag clatter to indicate an approaching train. High overhead are the signal flags.

In the cool shade of the trees at City Park one can watch the railroad crews disembark and carry their grip across the park to hotel. Here they spent the night and the next day leave the hotel, walk across the park to the depot and get ready to drive their train back home. Hugo was a division point and for years the scene of crew changes was repeated many times during the day.

Go up the street a couple of blocks and see the Hedlund house museum. Here is the home of the Hedlund's. The first person to received land patents for homesteaders. Built in the 1870's, the building has been well maintained and houses a good collection of artifacts from early day Hugo. There is a small ante room where one can do some research on local history and people.

There on main street the buffalo hunters are lined up with their trophies having their picture taken. Watch the cowboys ride their horses into the saloon for a drink and out the back door. Hear about the brawls in the pool halls. The wild west rode and walked the streets of Hugo.

18 Open space is all that left of the Bagdad siding and section house.

Bagdad

When the Kansas Pacific railroad built across Lincoln County, it would put in sites for Maintenance of the tracks. Bagdad was one such place. It was a section location for the Maintenance of Way gangs. It was in use by the railroad into 1950's.

Today it sits pretty much forgotten, a small dot on the map. According to the USGS map there were two locations for Bagdad, about a mile apart on the railroad Right of Way.

At Bagdad there probably was a section house, a couple of

sheds and miscellaneous out buildings. Here the railroad could stock materials and supplies for work on the ROW. Not much is said about this spot the railroad made. There is no mention if other people lived in the area or if there were stores.

Midway between Hugo and Limon is where Bagdad would have been located. CR 26 goes south of US 40 and 285. Southeast of this intersection is a stand of trees in a gully and on the knoll sits a ranch house. To the south of this ranch about a mile is the rough location of Bagdad. There is no access without crossing private property. Nothing remains to be seen but the ghosts of the occasional railroad worker passing by.

Prior to settlement there were massive herds of buffalo in the area. The sand creek has pools of water and there are buffalo wallows in the area. Indians would camp in the area hunting their mainstay, the buffalo. In some of the local museums can be seen collections of arrowheads found in the area.

Today the ghosts of Bagdad sit and watch the occasional train pass by and in the distance can be seen the highway as travelers whiz past. Cattle now graze on the buffalo grass in the area and breezes of days past ruffle the trees of the sand crick.

Figure 19 A railroad Maintenance of Way machine cross the county road.

Lake Station

Located on the Union Pacific Right of Way is Lake Station. This forgotten train town is probably the most inaccessible of the little towns the Kansas Pacific RR built in Lincoln County. Lake Station stretches across a variety of property lines.

South on CR 23 one comes to a railroad crossing. To the west about a mile is a stand of cotton wood trees and shrubs. This is roughly where Lake Station was.

20 Lake Station the scene of numerous Indian Attacks and the railroad located a depot and town here.

At this lost town is where the last major Indian attack in Eastern Colorado began. The spring of 1870 the rails of the Kansas Pacific had reached Kit Carson, Colorado. From here west the chief engineer and survey party had laid out the grade for the right of way. The engineer and survey crew had reached Lake Station and was camping there preparing to push on west. Behind them were work crews, building bridges and grading. Some crews over 100 men.

On a cool spring morning the Cheyenne Indians launched a series of attacks on the railroad crews from Lake Station all the way back to Kit Carson. Most of the Indian raids were 10-12 warriors. The chief engineer at Lake Station was killed along with several other workers. Many were injured and most were scared. The railroad crews beat a hasty retreat back to Kit Carson.

General Palmer, the construction manager for the railroad, did not like having his crews running like they did. General Palmer got on the telegraph to Washington DC demanding some kind of protection. The military responded by sending out General Custer. Custer and Reno went to Eastern Colorado and patrolled along the Kansas Pacific railroad looking for Indian trouble.

By the time Custer and his troops arrived the Cheyenne had moved north, to join up with the Sioux, to meet Custer on another day. After the arrival of the troops the Indian attacks in the area ceased. The railroad got more workers and another chief engineer. Westward the tracks continued.

Today the monster coal trains roll by, blowing their horn for the grade crossing ahead. Nearby can be seen a detachment of mounted blue coats watching.

The Rock

The truck load of wheat slowed down for the stop sign at the railroad crossing. Off in the distance the driver could see the headlight of the approaching train. Shifting to a lower gear, the truck eased up the rise to begin the bouncy ride over the rails. The crossing was pretty rough and the truck bounced around pretty good. Soon it was on the downhill side of the crossing. Pushing on the accelerator the truck grumbled into life to continue the journey to the grain elevator.

The bouncing stopped but the waving began, the driver heard a roar rush past the rear of his truck. Looking in the rearview mirror, all the driver could see was flashing sliver flying past. The truck was rocking from the wind of the *Rocky Mountain Rocket* as it flew down the rails at 80mph.

The crack passenger trains of the Rock Island kept a tight schedule as they carried passenger, freight and mail across the country. Shortly the *Rocky Mountain Rocket* would be stopping at Limon. Here would be the shuffle as the Rocket was broken into two sections. One section to Colorado Springs the other section to Denver.

When the *Chicago Rock Island & Pacific RR,* reached Colorado in 1888 it was building towns in hopes of customers. Many speculators had hopes that the railroad would use their town of dreams. The Rock Island had their own plans for where towns should be located and quite often the railroad and the speculators plans did not mesh. What had been communities closed or moved to be near a railroad stop. One such speculator guessed right, when he laid out his town, the following year the Rock Island built a stop at his town.

One Charles A Creel had came to Colorado, following the lure of the yellow rock. He was in Cripple Creek when he heard of the new railroad being built towards Colorado Springs. Mr. Creel packed up and headed back east. He set up a tent and platted out a town. Soon he was selling lots and the town of Arriba had its beginnings. On a high ridge above the rest, the little town took hold with the railroad making a stop there.

Charles Creel was a man of temperance and his town would not sell alcohol beverages. Yet there were those who had a yearning for liquid libations. Soon a man with a big thirst, bought some land next to Creel's and platted out another town, Frontier City. The first structure in this new town was a saloon, right across the street from Mr. Creel's home. A feud between the two towns broke out and lasted until the demise of Mr. Creel. In downtown Arriba today there is a marker talking about this alcohol dispute and the *No Man's Land* that was created because of it.

21 Blow dirt has buried the snow fence for the railroad, only the code poles remain.

Westward the construction of the new railroad continued. Soon it reached the rails of the Kansas Pacific. Here was the midway point between Goodland, Kansas and Colorado Springs, a good place for the railroad to build a division point. Construction was begun on a roundhouse, depot, hotel, office and related building. This railroad camp was named for a railroad foreman, Limon and became known as Limon's camp.

Soon a town started building around this camp, there were saloons, dance halls, livery and stores. No longer was it Limon's Camp it now was the town of Limon. The Rock Island built a good sized complex at this junction with the other railroad. Nearby was the town of Lake Station that the Kansas Pacific RR was using. Within a couple of miles of each other, there was a built in rivalry of these two towns. Because of its location and crossing of tracks and roads, Limon won out and Lake Station faded into the memory books.

Today one can visit the Limon Depot Museum and see many of the pictures from this early era. The ruins of the roundhouse and office building are now rubble piles between the legs of the wye that still get used occasionally today. To the west of the depot are the piers of the bridge that crossed the Big Sandy Creek. Here one can pause and look west, eyes following the old ROW, now a ghost trail.

Building towns was the focus of the railroad construction crews. They would put sidings in at about 5-6mile intervals. One such place crossed the Texas-Montana Cattle trail. Here there was good water for the railroad's steam engines. A siding was put in and a water tank built. The town was named for the thousands of cattle that passed trough, Bovina.

Bovina grew into a prosperous city of over 500 people. The railroad was important to the growth of the town. There were couple of small factories in town and it became a shipping place for cattle. With the depression and dust bowl, many little towns began to wither and Bovina was one of them. Residents began to leave, moving to other towns, businesses were closed and soon the railroad was removing the siding in town. No longer were cattle passing through, the train was no longer pausing for water and people were buzzing on by on the highway. In the 1960's the Interstate highway went through town, paving over lots of the town and some of the homes. No longer was Bovina, it is now only remembered by an exit sign on the Interstate.

The Chicago Rock Island & Pacific Railway grew to be one of the biggest railroads in the country. They boasted of over 10,000 miles of track, connections from coast to coast and border to border. Then in the 1950's the company made some bad management decisions. During the 60's the railroad could not recover from these mistakes and soon was in bankruptcy. With government agencies involved, the railroad continued to decline leaving the track in very poor condition. Soon it was beyond minor repair and to be used by other suitors and the Rock Island folded, becoming a chapter in the history books of railroading.

Parts of the old Rock Island were bought up and survive as parts of other railways. The Rock Island section in Colorado survived from Limon, CO east to Kansas. Their industrial areas in Denver and Colorado Springs are still used today by other rail companies.

22 The former Rock Island yard in Limon is still a busy place as the Genesse and Wyoming now operate over the tracks.

With an astute ear one can wander along the old tracks and still hear the whistle of the engine in the distance. See the smoke plums rising over the high plains.

Figure 23 A local plies the rails on the old Rock Island rails.

Saugus MP 503.6

When the Chicago Rock Island and Pacific Railroad constructed their railroad they were trying to create towns. For towns would provide customers for the railroad. When the Chicago Nebraska Kansas and Colorado Railroad, construction company for the Rock Island, began building west across the prairie to Colorado Springs, they were putting in sidings about every 5-6 miles in hopes that a town would develop. For the most part a town would grow around the railroad siding. Sometimes the railroad would plat the town and soon there would stores and businesses. Occasionally towns would not spring up and the railroad had nothing to look forward to.

Saugus was one such endeavor of the Chicago Nebraska Kansas and Colorado RR. At Mile Post 503 the company put in a siding. MP 503.6 became known as Saugus. Just west of the Lincoln County line at the eastern extremities of Interstate 70 Is where the community had its birth. Whizzing east on the Interstate one can blink once and miss Saugus twice.

The railroad tried to establish a town, they put in a depot, there was a store and a couple of residents. The life of Saugus was short lived. Soon the people moved to a neighboring town. The store rolled up its sidewalk and the railroad put its depot back into the depot box and shipped it off somewhere.

Today there is a farm overpass nearby and from this overlook one can see the signal post lying in the weeds, the concrete pedestal is overgrown but the MP sign still stands. In the distance one can see the tree line of neighboring Arriba. In Arriba are some real live west stories.

24 Just west of the county line is a barren weedy spot next to the tracks. Here the Rock Island wanted to build a town. The depot, store and other building have long been gone.

At Saugus not much happened and there still is not much going on. The railroad tracks still hear the occasional train rumble by and the wind of the Interstate whines as travelers fly by. It is a pretty forlorn place, surrounded by fields, the snow fence still covered in blow dirt, a big bird of prey circles overhead and the sound of the prairie icon the Meadowlark can be heard.

A signal maintainer form the 1800's can be seen at times moaning over his lost signal lamp. In the shadow of the overpass the hobo can be spotted camping for the night, small fire glowing, can of beans cooking and water for coffee boiling. Time has passed the burg by.

Arriba

A Tale of Two Towns

Across the prairie of eastern Colorado the Chicago Kansas and Nebraska was building a highway of iron. Many a speculator wanted the railroad to pass through their claim. Many a dream failed but a few were fulfilled.

25 **The town the the railroad built in conflict.**

A Charles A Creel had traveled to Colorado with the fever of gold. He had ended up in the gold fields of Pikes Peak at Cripple Creek. He heard about the new railroad being built across the high plains and headed for Colorado Springs. Mr Creel packed up and went back east. Out on the rolling prairie he bought a parcel of land and platted out a town in 1888. Sure enough, the following year the iron rails went through his town. The man who had set up a tent to sell lots in his town had guessed correctly where the railroad would pass.

Sitting on the high plains the new town was given the name Arriba for it sat above the prairie. The pronunciation was anglicized and is pronounced, Air..... baaah. Pronounce it the Spanish way and the locals look kind of cross eyed at one.

A depot was built by the railroad as were other structures. The town of Arriba was a going little town. There were shops, stores, banks, a newspaper, etc.

Charles Creel moved from his tent into a nice house in his new town. He was a temperance man and no stores selling alcoholic beverages were allowed. Arriba was growing and new people were arriving.

A CC Coleman moved to Arriba in the early 1900's. He was a hard working man that had a thirst. There being no alcoholic beverages nearby, he took matters into his own hand. Next to Arriba Mr Coleman acquired some land platted out a town.

In 1904, Frontier City came into existence and the first building in the new town was a saloon. The establishment was built right across the street from Mr Arriba's house, Charles A Creel's. That did not set very well with the founder of Arriba. The view from his yard or window was of a saloon. The gall boiled over and Charles Creel forbade residents of his town to partake of the saloon.

A fence was built between the two towns. Frontier City had what some of the people of Arriba wanted and the fence to not stop the thirsty residents of Arriba from Going to Frontier City's drinking establishment. Daily there would be holes in the fence to be repaired and daily a worker would go along and fix the fence up. Next morning there would be more work repairing the holes in the fence. A few said that George was making the holes at night so he would have work to do the next day.

26 Downtown Arriba's main street.

Seeing the fence was not very successful of stopping the thirsty residents of Arriba, Creel dug a ditch to separate the two towns. The ditch only slowed down the residents of

Arriba from going to the saloon. Soon the ditch became a trench and even that was not stopping the people of Arriba from going to Frontier City.

This trench became known as "No Man's Land." It divided the two towns. Each town had their own streets and businesses. Creel and Coleman kept up their feud, until Creel passed away. Mrs Creel did not like the feud and after her husband passed away, she met with Mr Coleman and settled their differences. The hatchet was buried. Frontier City became a part of Arriba.

The trench of *No Man's Land* remained and the street names did not change. Going East to West or vice a versa, when one crosses *No Man's Land,* the name of the street changes. Even today after 100 years the ditch is still there and the streets change names when crossing.

At twilight just after the sun sets the sharp eyed person can glimpse a shadow or two moving across *No Man's Land.* Quickly the shadows flit over the ditch that remains.

In downtown Arriba there is a sign marking *No Man's Land.* Here one can pause and look at the history of a town born of speculation, burned in animosity, pushed by desires, truly a town of the West.

Trains still pass nearby but the saloon is gone. The sound of tinkling glasses is a memory. A brief flash of light moves by, searching for a place of respite.

Bovina

Interstate 70 sweeps across the high plains of eastern Colorado, bypassing many a small town, the only memory of some of these little burgs is but an exit sign on the Interstate. The history of their names is as intriguing as the towns they once were. Bovina sits on a divide ridge between the Arkansas River and the Republican River watersheds. Here were small ponds and when the Texas/Montana Cattle Trail moved west these ponds became an important watering spot for the cattle being driven north.

When the railroad came through in the late 1800's, cattle drives were still passing by. The bovines by the thousands would be bedded and watered. So when the railroad platted out the town, it was named after the bovines, Bovina.

Today all that marks this important stop for the cattle men and the railroad is an exit sign, railroad crossing, old farm buildings and some old machinery. Cars go whizzing by without a passing thought, the occasional trucker pulls onto the exit ramp stopping for a quick forty winks and the big birds circle overhead looking for their next meal.

The westbound lane of I-70 went over the old Hwy 24 and covered the streets of the few people that had homes next to the tracks. The EB lane covered over what few highway businesses that were left. On the south side can be seen the remains of where the schoolhouse had been and the footers for a few houses. North of the railroad tracks is where the rest of the town was. Here are parked some old pieces of farm machinery, footers marking where buildings had stood, depressions of basements and assorted scraps.

Bovina was a major town in eastern Colorado in the early 1900's. They had two factories, making corn brooms and ice cream. There were banks, movie house, stores, shops, a post office and a thriving population of over 500 people. During the era of steam engines the Rock Island railroad would stop at Bovina to take on water.

During the Great Depression things began to change, then the Dust Bowl and the flood of 1935. Bovina was changing, people were leaving to go find jobs, stores and shops were closing and the school consolidated with a neighboring town.

On a quiet day one can pause at the exit ramp and hear the memories floating by, the low mooing of the cattle, the bleat of the train horn as it rumbles over the iron rails. Then reality hits, the rushing wind of the big rigs flying past.

The town of Bovina is still platted and people still own lots in the town that now boasts of more ghosts then residents.

Park on the frontage road, hear the laughter of children playing in the school yard that used to sit on the south side of town. Listen to the cars whiz by, the cattle herd is kicking up dust to the north as they move on. People load cartons of freight at the broom factory for shipment on the railroad. The ice cream factory sends out cartons. The bankers are prosperous and visit with the town merchants on the north side of the rails. During the early 1900's this was a center of commence on the high plains.

Sunday afternoon after Church one can see a few of the locals waking the field north of town looking for arrowheads. That evening they would be sitting around the front porch visiting about their day.

From a time that has passed, today is but a wide spot and exit on the speedway.

27 The Tower, a landmark on the highway, is just west of Genoa

Genoa

As the Chicago Kansas Nebraska and Colorado Railroad continued building westward they came to the pinnacle of Genoa. Here was advertised the highest point between Kansas City and Denver. Out on the escarpment one could look forever, well so it seemed. To the west rose the majesty of Pikes Peak, below was the broad expanse of the Big Sandy valley, all round spread the short grass prairie. The view was unsurpassed, it seemed there was no limit on what one could see from on top of the world here.

28 One of the town parks

Railroad workers would pause on the ridge taking in the view. Below them the railroad was putting in a siding at a place called Creech. Creech was the name of a Rock Island executive. A boxcar was placed at the west end of the flats for a depot. Soon there was a town platted out and businesses were established.

Creech was not a popular name for the new town and it was renamed by Cable. The popularity of Cable was even less. When the town folks heard that a railroad worker was hurt in an accident and was dying, Cable became short lived. The railroad worker was from Italy and he told his fellow workers he did want to die here, he wanted to go home and be in his home town of Genoa, Italy.

To honor the dying man the town name of Cable was changed to Genoa. The name stuck and has survived a century.

The new town of Genoa grew and prospered, a bank, newspaper, grocery stores, hotels, blacksmith, boarding houses, hardware, moving picture house and gas stations were built. Settlers were moving in and homesteading, the railroad was busy with the new little town named after one of their workers hometown.

With the advent of the horseless carriage a new American tradition popped up, a roadside attraction. That ridge that has such a great view was also a bane for the early American automobile traveler. Up and down the Genoa hills the puddle jumpers would struggle, Many times overheating when they got to the top of the hill. An entrepreneur set up shop at the top of the last hill. Here travelers could pull in and service their struggling car and maybe spend some money. A tower was erected, advertising that six states could be seen from the top. Genoa was on the map with its own tourist trap.

Today the Tower is still open but Genoa has rolled up its sidewalks. Town Hall is open part time, there is a Post Office and a grain elevator. Walk down the street, the hotel is shuttered, the bank is a residence, the tractor store is falling down, the drug store/grocery is in jeopardy of collapse and there are numerous abandoned buildings in town.

The shadows of days past flicker and float on dusty streets, the occasional well groomed yard, blooming flowers, inviting playground with picnic tables, a town with ghostly memories.

Pause on main street, listen to the wind talk about business deals at the old hotel, the drummer boy pedaling his pots and pans, the gypsy barn painters in town, the Tin Lizzie sputtering steam as it passes the horse and buggy. Farmers in town for Saturday shopping, carts dropping off cream cans at the RR depot, the steam engine wheezing as it waits, life in the small town was different in days past.

Mustang MP 526.1

Out in the middle of nowhere close to somewhere the Chicago Kansas and Nebraska railroad put in a siding called Mustang. Being on the face of a ridge it was a difficult terrain to build on. The ridge that the railroad crossed just west of Genoa made for difficult travel. The railroad did lots of cut and fill to level out the hills they crossed but here there was a good grade. The Genoa hill was a torment for man and beast to cross. The grade for the railroad was over 1%, making it a tough ridge to climb. The diminutive engines of the 19th century would need help getting up hills of more than 1%.

29 A train rounds the curve at Mustang on the climb to Genoa.

The siding at Mustang became a helper station. The gullies and ridge were too steep to build many structures on. A depot was built and at the east end of the siding was a small pond. Here the helper engine could get its orders for return or pushing. Shoving the train up the hill was an adventure years ago.

Speed could get out of sync, things could break and mishaps were not uncommon. Once over the rise at Genoa the helper would un couple and return to Mustang for another job or go back to Limon and the roundhouse.

There is a farm road that goes across the railroad tracks just north of the Interstate. Just to the west of this crossing is an old signal lamp stand. This approximately where the siding would of been located. Here one can pause and listen to the steam pistons working as they climb the grade. Black smoke belching from the stacks of the tiny engines, the depot agent stands on the platform watching the spectacle. Later years when the highway was built the Genoa Wonder Tower would dominate the eastern horizon.

It was a page in history that merited a sentence or two. Today it is but a passing thought of yesteryear.

Chronicles

Lincoln County

Ulysses

In 1894 Ulysses was established, there is no mention of what was there. It is a dot on the USGS map. It would have been along old highway 24 where it junctions with highways 40 and 287. Today it would be under the exit ramps of Interstate 70 where it crosses this junction.

30 Ulysses was probably a speculators dream that the railroad bypassed on their way to the KP junction.

Speculation would be that a speculator wanted this place to become a railroad town. The Chicago Rock Island railroad was building across Kansas, headed for Colorado. There were many speculators that set up trading posts in hopes the railroad would stop at their place of business. If that was the case, the people of

Ulysses were disappointed for the railroad went on west and set up camp at Limon.

Almost due south was the railroad town of Lake Station, roughly 4 miles. Someone from here may of seen the advance of the railroad and seen what he could profit from if he had a town on the new railroad.

To start a business in the late 1800's required a tent of sorts and a sign. Travelers would stop if they needed supplies or information. One such enterprising gentleman set his tent up along the stage route. He hung his sign that said trading post. The travelers stopped there to get some food. They entered the tent asking for something to eat. He had some molding pork fat, well dried hardtack and stale flour. He did have some barrels of whiskey though. He offered it to the travelers, saying it was the finest west of the Mississippi.

Now under layers of sand, gravel, concrete and asphalt lies the forgotten spot of Ulysses. Flying over the interstate speedway one probably dives over what had been the dream of an enterprising gentleman. His ghost probably sits in the shade of the exit signs watching the high speed travelers flash past, not knowing what they are passing.

The Ghosts of Limon

Limon is not a ghost town but it has more then its fair share of ghostly tales. When the Chicago Kansas and Nebraska built across the Kansas Pacific Railway they set up an area full of myths and other tales.

The space between the converging rails became a place of story fields. Here one could pause and watch the lights float over the field, see the fires of the hobos, listen to the outlaws plan their next robbery and other shady dealings bounced around.

Even today, the area just south of the old Rock Island tracks known as *Hollywood,* is supposed to harbor ghosts. Many a younger couples have taken advantage of the empty area and have returned the next day to school with stories of strange happenings.

When the Rock Island railroad crossed the rails of the Kansas Pacific there was nothing in this area, it was open grassland. The depot for the KP was over that a way a couple of miles. Here on the banks of the Big Sandy Crick the new railroad set up camp and named it after one of the local workers.

This new railroad was not new to robberies, Jesse James had them for a notch back east. Experience with outlaws was nothing new but to set up on haunted pastures was something new. From the beginning there were gremlins floating around Limon's camp. Fires started, depots burned and equipment disappeared. Workers were scared off. Lights floating over the barren grasses did not set well. The myth of Limon's camp was growing.

Today the stories are there but quietly whispered for fear of angering the gods of myth.

Along the banks of the crick can be found small camps, here the bums and hobos pause briefly. There are marks/signs that are tagged on walls, piers and other places indicating what is available in Limon, food, clothes, shower and whether the local police will hassle them.

These passing wayfarers create more stories adding to the myth. Separate out the reality, was it ghosts or a transient?

Hollywood is where the Rock Island built their roundhouse and other structures. One can pause next to the yard and look across the tracks and see rubble piles of the remains of these buildings. Here men lived out their lives working for the railroad. Today it is the spirits of these men that make the clanging sounds that roll out of the rubble piles. The occasional train uses the wye to circle around the rubble pile to turn their engines.

Figure 31 The Operation Lifesaver train awaits passengers in Limon.

Nearby are the remnants of bridge piers sitting in the sand crick. Standing on the banks by the depot one can look off in the distance to Pikes Peak and hear the roar of the trains pounding the now gone iron rails. The Rock Island, She was a mighty fine line, as the song goes. No longer do the Rockets zip over the rails. Today it is but ghostly memories gliding on the high iron.

Gone are the majestic hotels, the railroad worker trodding up the rise for a night's rest, the lonesome whistle no longer flying over the prairie or black smoke arching high over head, a time that has been lost. In the myths of stories is a flicker. Are the lights a railroad worker walking from his train, maybe a worker headed for the roundhouse or is it an outlaw looking for the loot he stashed.

Myths abound in Hollywood. The fallen railroad lamented. Ghost trains on the high iron. Hobos waiting for a slow train to pass, new bums hopping off the train to go in search.

Lincoln County

Smoky Hill Road

The dust could be seen in the distance, gently rising into the calm air. Across the treeless plains one could see for miles. There on the ridge could be seen the outlines of wagons, drifting down the slope for the springs. A small oasis on the prairie, where travelers could pause, get water and camp for the night. It had been a stage station earlier and the adobe walls of the buildings and corrals could still be seen. To the west rose the blue grey peak, their guidon to the Rocky Mountains. Pike's Peak had been the dominant feature on the western horizon the past days. Each passing day it grew closer, its snow capped slopes a faint hue of pink in the morning to a brilliant white later in the morning to a bluish cast that afternoon.

The Smoky Hill Trail was the shortest route from the Missouri river to the gold fields of the Colorado. It was the fever of gold that lined the trail west. The Indians had been following it for centuries and when the Europeans showed up the trail was marked partly by the Indians.

The French had traveled up the Missouri River and then followed the rivers westward across Kansas in search of fur and wealth that was in the new land. The rivers were the express way used by early French trappers heading into the Rocky Mountains.

When the United States made the Louisiana Purchase, lots of the trails were already in place. A Frenchman, Bourgmont had explored along the Smoky Hill River to its head waters in eastern Colorado. When Lt. Zebulon Pike was given the assignment to explore the new acquisition of the US he had some Indian guides to lead him. From Ft Leavenworth, Lt Pike began his journey westward, following the early trails along the rivers. He traveled the Kaw River to its junction with the Republican River and the Smoky Hill. Here he rambled across both rivers back and forth. He did not keep the best records during his exploration and where he traveled is up for debate. Yet across eastern Colorado did he roam. His destination was the mountain that would soon bear his name.

Out of this auspicious beginning was the trail along the Smoky Hill River begun. Gold seekers had been wandering this area from the first strike in California. In 1859 with the reports of gold in Colorado the rush was on to get the Smoky Hill route going. It was the shortest distance to the goldfields of Pikes Peak.

Surveyors were sent out to plot the road, set markers and help locate water. The gold fever was boiling, people began pouring across the plains of eastern Colorado, walking, pushing wheelbarrows, dragging hand carts or traveling with an oxen team and wagon. Many travelers would get lost, roam in circles, not find water and run out of food. The buffalo had liked the dirt mounds the Army had put up to mark the trail and they using them as wallows.

Lincoln County

East of present day Hugo, Colorado, branches of the Smoky Hill Trail joined together. The South branch followed the Big Sandy Creek. To shorten the trail a north branch was made, going cross country miles north of the Big Sandy. Roughly 5 miles east of Hugo, the two branches joined into one trail to roll down to Willow Springs. Here there was water and good grass and a place to camp. Later Willow Springs become a stage station. The Smoky Hill Trail wound north of Hugo to avoid the steep hill climb and crossed hwy 109 at about the golf course, North of Barron Springs.

Hugo was the early day pioneer crossroads of the prairie. Here, stage lines met and crossed the Smoky Hill Road. It was a junction for travelers. Today many of these paths are but memories lost, to be hinted at in history.

Westward the trail rolled to Lake Station. Here the trail divided again into South and North branches. Going straight west the south branch ambled across the prairie to meet the Big Sandy Creek. The north branch headed northwest to cross over the Cedar Point Ridge. Here the militia had established a fort to protect the travelers on the trail. Lincoln County sat in the middle of trails crossing and dividing, becoming one trail for a brief distance only to branch off to other ways.

Not much left to follow along today. Lots of the old trail is covered over or reclaimed by nature. Here and there one can see ruts from the wagons. CR 2R that goes straight east from the former Lady Bird rest area, kind of parallels the trail. East and north a couple of miles was Coon Springs, a few trees and wind break in the ranchers pasture. Coon Springs would be a stage station for a brief time. Further east, north of the road is Hugo Springs. There is a windmill out in the pasture in the general vicinity of the springs. These springs were important stops for the early day travelers. Going on eastward the slope rises up out of the creek basin. Looking back westward one gets wide view of the Pike's Peak on the far horizon. Here one can pause and gaze out over the roiling pastures, watching the gold seekers shuffle over the plains. On a good day one just may hear the mooing of cattle for the massive cattle drives from Texas to Montana passed through this area in the late 1800's.

Lincoln County

Silence now shrouds the land, occasionally the wind whistles over the timeless landscape. No longer is the creak of the wagon wheels heard, the shout of the stagecoach driver, the crack of the bull whip from the freighter, silent are the yips of the drivers pushing the cattle northward. It is a land empty, full of memories.

The main Smoky Hill Trail wound through central Lincoln County. To the north was the Benkelman cutoff of the Smoky Hill. Some travelers took the Republican River into Nebraska and at Benkelman they followed the Arickaree River to Cedar Point Fort. It is a long forgotten trail that brought many a settler into Colorado.

Along The Ghost Trails

The wheels groaned and creaked as they made the steady trek up to the ridge. The wagons stretched out across the face of the ridge as they moved under the high sun of the rolling prairie. Dust hung next to wheels, popping up in little puffs. The day was one of magnificence; a dead calm was the breeze. To feel a breeze one had to rush across the plains. On the north side of the wagons tread the wagon masters, staying in the shade. The sun was moving high and shortly they would be stopping for noon. A time to take care of the draught animals, feed and water them.

On a clear day, one can sit on the grasslands and watch the ghosts of wagon trains pass on the waves of the prairie mirage. Numerous trails crossed Lincoln County, bringing the gold and fortune seekers west. There were the stage routes, freight roads, military routes and wagon roads. SH 63 follows along the eastern edge of Lincoln County and crosses most of these phantom trails. SH 63 is a north south state route and a well maintained gravel country road. It has it curves and dog legs yet it is an adventure awaiting the traveler.

At the north end of the county, the state road crosses the Arickaree River. Paralleling the Arickaree was the Benkelman cutoff of the Smoky Hill Trail. Today the Arickaree doesn't look like any more than a dry sand creek. Over a century ago it was a small river carrying water to join the Republican River. Following this trail, early travelers were assured of a good water supply. It was still in use into the 1930's. A few of the old timers can remember seeing a few people traveling and they also can point out where a few ruts remain from this obscure trail.

Further south on SH 63 at the Jct. with I-70 is the town of Arriba, the town of two cities and a forlorn mansion.

Traveling on south on Hwy 63 one crosses the Leavenworth and Pikes Peak stage route and freight trail. CR 2Z goes east for a bit, paralleling the old stage road. Some place through here is where a stage station had been. Most people say the stage station was south on SH63 at an old abandoned house. When one looks at the creek that parallels CR2Z through this area, there are numerous springs and a few trees. Each of these areas would make a nice stage station. Where Station 22 was located is not definitive, makes for some myths.

Here one can pause and visualize the long freight trains rolling up the hill. Many of these freight trains would number over 100 wagons and many doubled up, pulled with 3-6 yoke of oxen. There were riders herding the extra oxen and relief drivers for ones that got sick. The stages would gallop along this trail, headed for Denver. The stages would travel in pairs to help protect from Indian attacks. It is along this route that Horace Greeley traveled when he first came west. There were stories of numerous Indian attacks and run away stages that Greeley's traveling companion recounted.

Traveling on south on SH 63 one comes to a dog leg. In this area and on south a number of miles stretched the Texas

Montana Cattle trail. The massive cattle herds from Texas passed this area on their way north. To the north is the town of Bovina, it was named for the cattle herds that paused in the area. Some of these herds could number as many as 9000 head of cattle. As they traveled north they were always in search of water for the cattle. Sometimes the trail could be 15 miles wide, depending where water was.

Driving on south on SH 63 one climbs over a divide between the Republican River and the Arkansas basin. On this ridge one can see out over the Big Sandy valley. With some keen eyes, the ghosts of the covered wagons or cattle herds can be seen moving over the mirage waves of the prairie.

Just before the junction with CR 2R on the north side, the North Branch of the Smokey Hill Trail crosses SH 63. It was also used by the Butterfield Overland Dispatch and Wells Fargo stage lines. Looking down the hill a ways can be seen a windmill. In this area would have been Hugo Springs, a stop on the stage line. The pioneer road went straight across the land to join with the South Branch of the Smoky Hill Trail east of Hugo. To the northeast of the Lady Bird, on US Hwy. 40 rest area is another stage stop, Coon Springs. There are some trees in the area and occasionally ponds in the creek. To the south was Mirage, a stop on the south branch. Here there is a live stream and a grove of trees.

Many of the old stage stations were difficult to pinpoint because of their construction and short lives. The early stations were built in 1860 and closed a few years later. The railroad eliminated the stage lines through the area when the rails were completed in the mid 1870's. Most of the stations were built of adobe or dugouts into the hillside. The corrals were sometimes referred to as mule cellars, being built into the hillside or dug outs. There were tunnels connecting the corrals and other structures because of the numerous Indian attacks. Some of the stations built small forts. A small hole was dug and then thatched with twigs, grasses and mud. Small slits were in the adobe blocks for gun ports and there was a water barrel in this dug out pit. It was connected to the house by a tunnel.

The remains of these structures have disappeared over time. Being on private property, the stations are not easy to access. A few locals have been able to take metal detectors and search some of the areas, with permission. They have found spent rifle cartridges and metal buttons in the area where the stations were suspected of being. The stage stations truly are ghosts floating over the plains.

Moving on south on SH 63 and crossing US Hwy. 40/287, one comes to the ghost town of Boyero. Boyero was a railroad town. It was the railroad that gave it life and it was the railroad that gave it ghosts. Boyero had been a fair sized community on the Golden Belt Route, until the highway was rerouted. There are a few buildings still standing and some hardy residents that keep the ghosts company. Some streets are still visible and the roadway follows along the railroad tracks. Here there was also a stage stop on the South Branch of the Smoky Hill Trail.

The Kansas Pacific Railroad made Boyero a major stop along their line. With the nearby stage line stop, there were numerous Indian attacks in the area, on the stage stations and the railroad workers.

Today it is the whirlwinds that stir up the dust. A few cattle graze nearby, the buffalo are gone but there are deer and bald eagles in the woods of the Big Sandy. Here one can catch glimpses of numerous birds, the darting merlin, the soaring prairie falcon, chirping meadow larks, gimp winged killdeer or the darting swallows or flycatchers.

Walks Camp

Colorado state highway 71 has a major course correction on the north end of Lincoln County. On the east end of this correction line curve, CR 3T goes behind the farmhouse on the corner. Going east on this country road takes one to an oasis of the high plains. Here is Walks Camp. Driving down the road 3T one could be startled at the roof line that rises over the ridge. For on second look it is not a barn or shed sticking up above the rise, it is a grandstand roof line.

32 The grandstand built in the 1920's still stands.

What is that doing out here in the middle of somewhere but close to nowhere. First thought would be a rodeo arena out in the country. Go down to the intersection with CR 27 and north a bit for a closer look and there it is, a huge old grandstand looking out over the pasture. It is not a rodeo arena but a ball field. Pulling in the parking lot and closer examination one can see the plow discs that mark the bases, the pitcher's mound is flat and bare, home plate is marked by a couple of barren depressions and the base paths are overgrown with buffalo grass. Nowhere close by are any towns yet there it is, a onetime grand ball field.

Walks Camp got its beginnings back in the early 1870's. A German Baron came over to the America's for a buffalo safari. Along with his entourage the German went to Denver, got outfitted for their buffalo safari and took the train out east to hunt buffalo. They unloaded their gear and equipment from the train and headed for the high country around the head waters of the Arickaree River. A level spot protected by ridges, a few trees and water was located. Here Herr Walks set up camp for his buffalo hunting expedition. For a few years other hunting parties ventured into the area and camped here. It became known as Walks Camp.

Soon the buffalo were gone and settlers were moving in. Homesteads were filed, homes were built, schools established and churches built in the area. Walks camp was a nice area and settlers would go to this area for gatherings on the summer holidays. Baseball was popular game at the turn of the previous century and at these picnics a baseball game would happen.

Some of the early pioneers got together and decided to build a nice ballpark with a grandstand. Construction began and out of the pasture a grandstand arose. School children would have school picnics there and they would plant trees in the newly built park. The Arickaree was a small stream and provided good water for the trees. The school children would dig a hole for their tree. They would also have a small glass jar and put their name in the jar. Along with the tree, this jar with their name in it was planted with the tree. Today the park has a good sized grove of trees along the creek.

For the national holidays of the summer, people would travel to Walks Camp to celebrate. There would be plentiful food, deserts, games, fun, visiting and there always the ball game.

The crack of the bat, cheers from the seats, running, yelling and the inevitable discussion, was he out or safe. Baseball on the prairie was a pastime that had no peer. Here it was to have fun. There were no fancy baseball gloves, sometimes no gloves at all, maybe a work glove to ease the shock some. If the bat broke, get the friction tape out, pound a nail or two in and tape the bat up, batter up. A new ball was rare, usually a few years old and maybe a torn seam but the game went on. Bases were improvised but accurate, the ball field was set up correctly, all the dimensions were accurate, it was a big league ball filed in the pasture. No, there were no cow chips in the field.

Shaw

To the north end of Lincoln County lies the little community of Shaw. Here there was a General Store, Gas Station, a Post Office and other buildings. At the junction of CR 4C and CR38 is a few trees, some footers, a corral and small sheds. Not much else as reminder that this was once a busy little burg on the prairie.

Nearby are a variety of abandoned buildings, mostly homesteads. It is surprising to see so many still standing. Because of taxes many of these abandoned dreams have been torn down. Yet one can see how many people lived in the area at one time and there would be a small community in the area.

33 One of the few homesteads that still stand in the area.

Daily the letter carrier would bring the mail up for the people and the mail to be delivered back to the Post Office would be picked up for the railroad to gather. It was a scene that was lived out until the mid 50's when the Post Office was closed. Soon the store would follow along with the gas station. What had been a bustling little community was going into the memories of a few locals. No longer was the community barn used for dances, card parties, quilting bees, weddings or get together. Today the corner lot sits vacant, memories float among the grasses, cattle graze where people had lived their lives.

On a warm summer day a cloud of dust can be seen in the distance. The approaching car can be made out. It is the letter carrier bringing the mail. In her front seat the letter carrier has a couple of packages of baby chicks chirping. The clanking of cream cans can be heard bouncing out of the back seat mixed with the mail pouch back there. The letter carrier was also a neighbor and she would help her neighbors by carrying packages to town or carrying the cream cans to and from the train station .

34 A depression, a reminder of where a home once stood.

At the store she would exchange pleasantries with the store keeper and who ever happened to be in the store that day. The letter carrier that delivered on north would be there and together they would sit at the little table and sort out the mail in the corner of the store. Finished putting the mail up then they would get in their cars and continue their routes. Dust swirling up from the road, cream cans rattling, baby chicks chirping. The mail would be delivered.

No longer does the tinkle of the piano roll out the barn door, the call of the square dance is silent, and no longer do people meet in the community barn. The community dance hall was transported to another town, way over there.

Today these memories float over the plains, ghosts of times past. Some of the locals remember those days and still say they are going to Shaw. Well, that's where their farm land is.

Lincoln County

Wellons

There in the furrows of a field is where a building once stood that housed a Post Office. Wellons was a Post Office in 1908 and more than likely was the home of a farmer. During the early 1900's the Post Office would contract with farmers and ranchers to operate a Post Office for them. On occasion these would turn in to a community and maybe grow to a small town.

35 What had once been a Post Office is now a field.

In the case of Wellons it appears not much happened at the Post Office. There were no notes how long the office life was. Sometimes the farmer would not like the idea after all of having people enter his house to transact business of getting mail or mailing letters. So they would let the contract expire or quit and a new place would be found.

Going north from the ghosts of Sagus on CR 48 one will come to a bend in the road. Here at this bend is where the USGS map locates

Wellon. A short distance beyond the intersection of CR 4U in a farmer's field is where the map shows it to be. Nearby is a windmill, otherwise the land is devoid of any other structures. One can only imagine what it would have been like in 1908 to carry the mail out to this now empty field.

Over 100 years ago there were few fences and the wagon roads meandered, following the easiest route. Out there someplace stood a building that the wagon would be headed for. Did it climb over the rise to drop down the hill to the settlers place? The nearest town is about 12 miles away on the railroad line. It would have been a full days ride out and back for the delivery. Were other things delivered? Was it a trading post or store or shops. The mysteries of ghosts leave so much to be conjured up.

The City of Gold

Sitting on the escarpment overlooking the river basin the figure sat looking to the far southern horizon. Dust swirled up, moving his direction. It was unusual for the dusty line stretched out behind and slowly drifted off towards the sun. The buffalo herd he had been searching for was behind him, grazing on the mesa. Soon he would drop off the ridge and follow the creek back to the village where his family was. For now he was content to sit and watch the moving dust cloud.

The cloud moved closer so that he could see shapes moving in the hazy cloud. Finishing up lunch he moved down a gully and headed in the direction. The sun overhead was cool, the heat of spring was but a hint. Taking long strides he moved across the land, dropping into a wash and climbing up the other side. There on the ridge he could see in the distance again and the dusty cloud now had clear shapes in it. None of which he had ever seen before. There were men walking with long lances and had shiny objects on their head reflecting the sun. Beside them were other men, sitting on animals he had never seen before. Behind them were other animals pulling wagons that creaked and groaned as the wheels rolled over the prairie.

The Arapahoe Indian stood in amazement at the scene that was unfolding before him. Never before had he seen such animals and to see them pull a home behind them. Then there were the people in the shiny helmets and long lances. Where had these people come from. Out in front he saw some Indians like he had seen from before. His family and other members of the tribe had traded with them along the river, in the "Tall Timbers." What were they doing with these strange people and animals.

The procession slowly moved towards the nearby spring and in the direction of his village. The Arapahoe gathered himself and began a brisk lope to home and to report to the elders what he had seen.

It was 1540 and Coronado was in search of the cities of Cibola. In the southeastern corner of Lincoln County, it is suspected that the El Cuartelejo may have been located in this area, one of the cities of gold. This area was home to some Indian villages along the creeks that crossed through the area and this may have been the guise the Indians of New Mexico used to lure Coronado out of their homeland.

This band of conquistadores would change the life of the plains Indians. The Europeans brought with them horses. It was also a new group of people moving on the plains. Soon there would be more of them crossing the prairie of the Indians. The trails of the local inhabitants would soon become the trails of the newcomers. The Spaniards relied on the guides to show them the water, where to travel and live on the grasslands. It was the opening chapter of a new life for the Aboriginals who lived on the prairie. Soon there would be more Europeans exploring the New World. They too would use the skills of the Indians to guide them across the plains.

The southern edges of Lincoln County are wide open. Not many ranches or farms, no villages, for the Indian are long gone. There are few roads into the area and one can easily get turned around. For the adventurous soul it is a place where time is on pause. Here one can see a land that has changed little. Cattle graze on the grass, the occasional home stands out and the creeks turn green with trees in the spring. It is a land where the wind eases through the grasses or roars with the storms to become a quiet moment where one can hear life move.

Where were the Indian villages. Not much reminder of where they had been. Artifacts are found here and there. No record was kept of these findings. It is only speculation where they were. The wail of a squaw lamenting over a lost past can be heard across the land. The Indian brave trotting along the creek is seen at times. The buffalo can be found in a pasture, easily grazing on its namesake. Here is a place where one can wander and not see much but open space and search out the ghosts from the past.

Damascus

In the southeastern corner of Lincoln County was the Post Office of Damascus, interesting name for an obscure place on Rush Creek. The Post Office was established in 1914. Nearby was the country school of Prairie Grove. How the name Damascus came about is a bit of a mystery. A few old timers can tell one where Damascus was but not much more. It does raise some speculation on how the name came to be.

As obscure as the location was, it is an adventure of getting there. No roads lead to the site. At the end of CR43 there is a pasture gate, covered in tumble weeds and ruts beyond leading towards Rush Creek. Nearby is a ranch house and it more than likely in their pasture where Damascus once was.

36 A lone building stands a far distance in a pasture.

The USGS map shows a wagon road passing through the area, following Rush Creek and it may have been the road that served the Post Office. In the area is an old stucco style building in the far reaches of a pasture. It doesn't look like a typical home. Has more of an appearance of a commercial building. Sitting next to the wagon road raises questions of what it was used for.

So many ghosts roam the area and they beg so many questions. How busy was the road, what kinds of businesses were on it, who were the travelers or was it a road for the post office to travel?

Bouncing over a bridge a small herd of deer are startled and bound up over the fence across the road. Here in the little gullies small water pools can be found. Wildlife finds these watering holes and congregating around them, seldom disturbed by travelers. Down in the trees of Rush Creek in the shade on a warm sunny day a variety of wildlife can be seen basking in the shade of the woods. The ghosts of the Indians that roamed in the creek do not bother the wildlife. Today it is cattle that keep the grass shorn. No longer do the buffalo roam over the prairie. Birds flutter by, dust swirls up from the passing of the winds of time.

37 Somewhere beyond the ranchers gate was the Damascus Post Office.

Green Knoll

Next to CR F near the intersection with CR 34 in south central Lincoln County is Green Knoll. Here there was a country school and a Post Office was established in 1917. One can almost drive past the little knoll where the school once stood. There are some footer's and foundations plus some rubble at the site of this community. Just off the road in a ranchers pasture one can see a few remains of the buildings.

In the area are a couple of ranch houses, otherwise it is wide open country. Cattle graze the area now and the occasional antelope herd passes by. Not many places in the shade for ghosts to slumber and pass the time of day. Yet here in the area dreams were lived. Hopes grew strong for the settlers. Here they had their dream, of owning a piece of land in America.

**38 Footers are all that remain where the country school for the community
stood.**

A school house was built. Children learned, played and grew
up on the open prairie. This was their home. There were
weddings, picnics, funerals and weekend dances. Today the
ghosts languish in nearby abandoned homestead where there are
trees to shade them.

On the knoll, a rubble collection is a mute memorial to times
past. Here one can pause and wonder what one seen in the land.
What brought the early settlers to such a stark landscape? Those
that pause can hear the siren song of the land. Here one can
watch the birds float over head, see the grasses to graze cattle on,
dirt to raise a garden in, a piece of land one could call their own.

Karval

Across the prairie a grove of trees reaches for the clouds, roof lines peeking through the leaves. On down the country road a small farming community comes into view. Trees line the streets, buildings scattered along the roadway. Some are still in use a few are abandoned. The flag flutters over the Post Office, couple of pickups parked in front of the coffee shop, the pulse of Karval moves.

39 **One of the old buildings in town, now a vacant lot.**

Farming/ranching communities were quite common in the early 1900's. They served the local settlers with basic necessities. In the day of horse and wagon, travel at 4mph, an all day trip was arduous. A short distance trip saved time for the early day settlers. Here they could shop, visit and take care of business.

With the changes in transportation many of these wide spots faded back into the grasses. No longer was travel at 4mph. The horseless carriage could fly over the puddles and be to the big towns by the railroad tracks in no time. Over the years the people of Karval have hung on to their community.

The school still teaches students and the post office still handles mail. Most of the other businesses have vacated. The empty buildings are reminders of when it was a bustling community. Stores are closed, the station is gone, garage shuttered up and vacant lots now house the memories of other days. The community building still hosts a variety of events, most notable is the Plover Festival.

The Rocky Mountain Plover, looks like a Killdeer, migrates through the area on the way to its summer and winter habitat. Early spring the birds are moving and some of the local ranches open up for tours to search out the elusive bird.

During this time the ghosts of main street settle down and are pretty docile. Country hospitality takes over the town. Breakfast is served, music peels over the plains and the ghosts tap their toes.

Situated in southern Lincoln County, Karval is not on any highway. It is in a ghostly location that takes some searching to find, or just follow the signs. Here one can stand on the ridge and see to eyes end, the air is cleaned by the breezes of the high plains and peace pauses for those who look.

Antelope herds boil over the ridge, fox surveys from his den, hawk circles overhead, deer seek the shade of cricks and the coyote ambles over the grassland. Here the west of old lingers. Cattle drives across pastures, roundups and branding, get along little doggies. Rounding bends in the road, what lies ahead.

Swift

Swift was a Post Office in 1910, not sure for how long but it appears it may have been in a ranch house. Swift is situated east of Karval, south of the junction of CR R and CR 38. The USGS map shows two locations on this half section of land. It is on private property and there are no remains in the field. There is a ranch house at the SW corner of the intersection

Here at Swift the neighbors could stop in, get the latest gossip, exchange pleasantries and take care of their mail. Weather is always a good topic in the country, how the crops are doing and how is the family. To visit for a spell in the country was a treat for many a settler. See how things are with their neighbors or get the news of goings on. Is there a quilting bee, maybe a dance that weekend, the new school teacher has arrived or maybe it is a new pastor.

Out in that open field there had been a home, outbuildings and life being lived out. It was a place of community. Pause, watch the wagon roll up to the house, listen to the exchanges of greetings. Sometimes it was weeks between visits to the post office. Lots could happen in between the visits.

Today the dust of ghosts swirl over the parched land, birds float overhead, perched on the fence post is the Meadow Lark, serenading the prairie. No longer does the bell of the country school house ring. Children now ride the bus to a neighboring town. Times past watch the yellow shadow of a bus slides into the horizon. Clothes on the clothes line, no longer flutter in the wind by the post office.

Here is the emptiness of dreams that were once. A silence settles over the land that can be heard beyond the rise. Hopes and dreams vanished, returning back to the earth.

Blue Cliff

On State Highway 71 is a sign for Blue Cliff, pointing east on CR J. Take the road up the hill, one does not come to a town but a country school house. It sits on the NW corner of the junction with CR 29. Blue Cliff school was built in the early 1900's to serve the people who had settled in the area and is still used by the local community today.

Drive on east on CR J, down the hill and turn around. Looking back up the hill one can see the cliff. In the early light of morning the mesa has a bluish cast and the sharp rise of the mesa lends it to looking like a cliff.

The ridge that sits over the basins of two drainage creeks is level making for good farm ground. In the area are numerous homes that have been there for decades. The little country school that many went to for early childhood learning now serves the neighborhood as a community building.

There are gatherings, weddings, funerals, potlucks or card parties. On Sunday the pastor from Hugo drives down to Blue Cliff for Sunday services. The ghosts quietly sit in the pews during the church service. The neighbors gather and celebrate their faith.

On a clear crisp fall day one can see the children walking to the school house. The teacher is standing in front, greeting the children and watching them as they play in the yard. Soon the bell will ring and there will be squeals and squawks as the children head into the school house for a day of learning. Later in the week, wagons will roll up for the weekend quilting bee. That evening the desks will be moved off to one side and the sound of the piano will fill the room as feet shuffle across the floor. The community passes the time visiting and living their lives.

High on the cliff that looks blue, people lived out their dreams, many have left, and some remain. The ghosts of other days silently sit nearby.

40 The former country school still stands on the corner. Once a week church is held here. It is also used for other functions.

Carr Crossing

Near the Intersection of CR 27 and CR D is the area of Carr Crossing. In this vicinity the USGS map lists three different locations for the Post Office. These locations are out in the pasture of a local rancher.

The 1914 location is NW of the junction about a mile, sitting near a draw. In 1917 the Carr Crossing Post Office moved to a location SW. It was situated on a road that connected the Kit Carson stage route to the Goodnight cattle trail to the Northwest. In 1920 the Post Office was moved again to a place NE of the intersection.

It is possible the different locations were houses of different settlers in the area and the Post Office retained the name Carr Crossing for the country school that was in the area. Many times the settler would leave or didn't want the Post Office any more.

Here along the ridge, elevation of about 5000 feet, one has a view to Pikes Peak. On a clear day the Peak looks out over the plains of southern Lincoln County. There are a couple of homes in the area, otherwise it is a clear vista out across the plains. Cattle drift over the grasslands grazing, a few antelope stand nearby. It is a land not much unchanged over the centuries.

The shadows of former times float over the trails crossing the area, dropping down into gullies, crossing dry creeks, climbing back up the hillside. There are a few relics in the pastures of where buildings once stood. Many of the early dwellings were dug outs or adobe. Not much remains of them. Occasional ruts can be seen on the grasses where wagons rolled.

Today the area of Carr Crossing is open land with an uninterrupted view over the prairie. Winds whispering, pushing the tumble weed over the land, birds sit on the fence row watching the traveler. No longer is the creak of the wagon wheel heard bringing mail to this outlying area almost due south of Karval. Schoolhouse is gone, no longer are the squeals of children echoing over the land. The ghosts of past days amble over the land, trails are covered, overgrown, long gone, memories are faint.

Wezel's

The wagon cracked and groaned as the animals struggled to get it through the sand creek. It was an easy crossing but the sand grabbed the wheels like glue holding tight. The driver was walking next to his team encouraging them on. Ahead and over there a bit was a barn and other buildings. Here the animals could be unhitched from the wagon, watered and allowed to graze by the creek. There were a few trees for shade from the late afternoon sun.

Louis Wezel had seen the approaching wagon as he worked around his yard doing evening chores. The driver walked up to Louis and said hi. Louis was asked by the traveler if it was okay to spend the night here as the sun was setting. Sure was the reply and Louis told him he could spend the night in the barn.

41 Wagon ruts across the pasture can still be seen.

In 1891 Louis Wezel immigrated to the United States and

found his way to Colorado. In south central Lincoln County he homesteaded. Little did he know that soon his place would become an early day version of barn and breakfast. Homesteading on the south banks of Rush Creek, close to the confluence of two branches, here it was an easy crossing for wagons headed north and south. The Wezel homestead was on the early day wagon freeway. As the travelers passed by they would pause for a spell to take care of their animals before climbing up out of the creek bottom. If it was late evening they would spend the night. Being neighborly, Wezel the settler offered his barn for the overnighters. In the morning, the travelers could have some biscuits and gravy.

Later the Wezel place would become a Post Office. Here the neighbors could stop by for a visit and send mail or pick their mail up. The little homestead that had humble beginnings in a dug out was now a post office and a place for travelers to pause for a bit of refreshment.

Today the homestead still sits on the bank of Rush Creek but empty. Louis Wezel's grandson now operates the ranch and a few decades ago a new home was built on the hill overlooking the creek. The homestead is now a ranch of over 3000 acres along parts of Rush Creek.

Along the banks of the creek one can still see some of the ruts from the wagons traveling through the ranch. As one trail up the hill became to worn a new path would be made beside .the old one. Across the pasture were a variety of traces going up the creek bank.

The Wezel's still have the little pigeon hole frame that was used to sort the mail and there are pictures of the building that was used for the Post Office. Today these are but dusty memories of another time.

The ghosts still urge their wagons up the hill and neighbors stop by to visit. As one crosses the 109 bridge on Rush Creek they can look east and see a grove of trees on the south bank. Here is where the homestead was. Wagons would pause nearby and horses would ride up for mail. It is a scene that floats over the sands of Rush Creek.

White's

North of SH 94 on CR 24 is the Post Office of White's. It had sat on the banks of the South Fork of Rush Creek. Today there is a corral where the map shows White's being located. Here one can pause and look out over the small valley and see the lure of the land, why people would settle here.

42 On the banks of the Rush Creef fork stood the White Post office. Near where the corrals are now.

Rush Creek has carved out a lush oasis, there are small pools, scattered trees and lush green meadows on the creek bottom. Swifts circle overhead putting on an aerial show capturing insects. Ducks float over the glassy sheen of the pond looking. Nearby, deer laze in the cool grasses during the heat of the day. On the far ridge can be seen the curious antelope, watching the strangers. A startled owl scurries out of its nest in the trees. The Western Meadow Lark serenades the onlookers. Bobolinks' are lined up on the barb wire, watching the tableau of the prairie unfold.

Here a settler had water, well watered grasses for grazing and nearby was level rolling land for farming. Today a ranch house sits on the north bank overlooking the creek.   To the far horizon the land rolled on forever, only the eye was the limit. To the west rises the majesty of Pikes Peak, snow capped peak looking out over amber waves on the high plains.

During the late 1800's this land would set a settlers heart ablaze. Here he could set down stakes and raise his family. Take his claim to nearby Hugo and file his patent at the land office in Hugo. Few years later, travel to Hugo and prove up his patent and the land was the settlers.

It was probably from Hugo that the mail for White's Post Office came from. Here the train stopped, delivering mail, supplies and other goods. A drayage service would carry the mail into the country among other goods. Places like White's would also have a small general store associated with their Post Office. Here the neighbors could pick up a few staples without going to town and exchange the local news.

White's Post Office probably became an Amy Post Office, considering the close proximity to the Amy community. White's may have also failed or left his settlement for reasons and somebody else got the Post Office.

There is nothing left of White's but the wonderment of earlier times. There were probably Indian camps in the area. After a Buffalo hunt the Indian families would camp out and process the buffalo, for their robes, jerky and pemmican, then move onto their homes. Let the mind wander over the land, what can be seen. Is it the wagon bringing supplies from town, the cattle grazing in the meadow, horses pulling the plow, it is a landscape awaiting the mind's eye. Rush Creek was the roadway of earlier days. Along its course there were other communities/Post Offices listed, Damascus and Wezel's. A wagon road followed the creek and there were early cattle drives over the land.

Punkin Center

One of the more famous little stops in Eastern Colorado is Punkin Center, located at the intersection of State Highways 94 and 71 in southern Lincoln County. Here there are no pumpkin patches but the junction has been referred to as Pumpkin Center.

In the early 1920's an adventuresome soul thought there should be a gas station at the intersection. So he built one along with a general store and coffee shop. The buildings were painted orange and over time faded to a pumpkin color.

This little business is where legends come from. The proprietor carried a gun for protection from thieves. But some thieves got the jump on him and tried to rob the establishment. He wrestled with the assailant and in the process got shot in the shoulder but he did best the thief. Wounded and bleeding the shop keeper drug the guy to the neighbors where the police were called. The other thief that got away was caught later.

Business continued at the country store for a number of years. Sometime later some youngsters out cruising needed some gas. They stopped to fill up and decided to rob the station. Being confronted by the robbers the store keeper reached for his gun but was not quick enough. He was fatally wounded and left to die as the crooks fled in their car.

The business was bought and stayed open for a number of years. The new owner was returning from the big city and he seen smoke on the horizon. Upon his arrival he saw that it was his store going up in smoke. The orange building had become a pile of ashes. It is said the first owner can be seen wandering the area searching.

Today the roar of tractors can be heard on a hot summer day as they charge down their course. Garden tractors roar to life for races and pulls throughout the summer.

No longer is there a gas station or a restaurant at the junction. There are a couple of homes and the Highway Department maintains a small shop.

Amy

Amy sits just east of SH 71 on CR2D. Here there is a stand of trees, a wind break and some cattle grazing. What had been there years ago is another thing. Looking at the map one could get the impression that Amy was on wheels and that every few years they would move Amy. Maybe that is why the Amy ghosts are so restless.

Across the road from the stand of trees is an occupied ranch house. Down the road around the corner is another location where Amy may have been. Here on this corner is an abandoned home and some rubble piles among the few trees. Then just ways further down the cross road is not much but a collection of trees, wheat fields and a large herd of antelope staring at the interloper. The antelope are a bit skittish as they eye the vehicle and the person getting out to take pictures. Off in the distance can be seen another old farm house sitting in the field.

The Post Office was relocated numerous times to other homes. There may have been a small store at one of the locations and nearby was the one room country school. There was a community center for dances, quilting, card parties and get together. Here families were raised and dreams were lived out.

Amy was a Post Office into the mid 1930's and a few old timers remember a bit about Amy. In the community was a mid wife. She traveled to neighboring areas to help the expectant mothers. One of the gentlemen that the mid wife had helped deliver him recounts the story of his father having to go and get the mid wife when his sister was due. He noted that it had just started to snow when Dad had to hitch up the wagon and go get the mid wife. By the time father had returned home four hours later the snow had turned into a storm. And the horses found their way home. The mid wife was snowed in there for a few days.

Mid wives were quite common on the prairie in the early 1900's. Up until the 1940's, WWII, they were still helping to deliver babies in their neighbor's home. Around the evening meals were many stories about their adventures on the high plains.

Pause by the empty tree stands, a wind break, listen to the conversations coming from the walls that once stood among the trees.

Owen

The Post Office of Owen was established in 1908. Being just a few miles south of Limon it probably was a ranch house to serve the neighboring homes. Not many of the old timers know about Owens. It did not have a long life as a post office and for that reason many memories of it were lost.

Today Owens is undergoing a bit of a revival. A local Co-Op is building a grain elevator in the vicinity where Owens had been located. If there had been any reminders of Owens, they are no more. The glistening steel grain bins cover most of the corner and the driveways have obliterated most of the rest. Then who knows, the granary may adopt the name of Owens.

The ghosts of this past century just may have a new home to hang out in. No longer do they have to sit in empty fields and watch the cars fly by on SH 71.

Owen is far enough south of Limon that a general store may of opened to serve the neighbors. Nearby were some one room country schools and the junction with CR 2W made a busy intersection.

Now the sound of grain trucks will be floating over the plains around Owen. During harvest the roads will be busy and when contracts come due. The old tyme ghosts will have something new to watch. No longer will it be the wagon and horses trotting up to collect the mail.

Sitting on a ridge Owen looks out across the valley of the Big Sandy and on clear days, Pikes Peak is visible. It is a commanding view from the ridge.

Surrounding the junction are fields and pastures. Nearby are a few farm homes and ranches. Sleepy days for the ghosts will be no more. Out of the ashes a new era begins for the lost community.

Four Corners

South of Limon on SH 71 was the community of Four Corners. Located at the intersection with CR 2Z. Four Corners may have been a collection of family homes that had a store or trading post. Four Corners still shows up on various maps as being a place, but today at this intersection is a farm house on the NW side. The adjoining corners are plowed fields. If there had been structures there they are long gone, plowed under.

On the near surrounding horizon can be seen other farm compounds and to the northwest, two and a half miles is a small country cemetery.

This empty land appears to of been a vibrant community at one time. Maybe even a gas station. Many pioneers settled among their countrymen and shared many interests.

One of the first things to be built was a schoolhouse or a church. Then it would become a community building. Sometimes it would be a barn. Here would be church, school, quilting bees, weddings, dances and meetings. Sometimes these buildings would be spread out in the area.

Many of these communities have faded into the ground and memories have become dim. Yet there are enough stories of other communities to patch together what Four Corners may have been like.

Today the cars and trucks on highway 71 zip by on their way to their destination. Not much waves back, the waves of grain flow in the wind, the corn reaches for the clouds and the occasional ghost stands on the corner.

Ghost Riders

Colorado State Highway 71 skirts along the western edge of Lincoln County. Towards the southern end of the county it crosses a couple of little known early pioneer roads, the Goodnight Cattle Trail and the Southern Overland Mail and Express route.

The cattle trail followed Horse Creek on its northwest route towards the gold fields of the Rocky Mountains. The mail and express company used the road from a military post a Kit Carson to Fort Reynolds, near Pueblo. These two roads cross the southern edge of Lincoln County where SH 71 has a correction dog leg at the south end.

Figure 43 A simple cross, a reminder of a grave.

Unless one has a good map the Southern Overland Mail and Express stage route, it is difficult to trace. It enters the southeastern edge of Lincoln County and wanders across the southern edge of the county to almost SH 71. There are no county roads to follow it by and it follows no water courses. It crosses Rush Creek on the eastern edge of the county, then across Adobe Creek in the south central part of the county and exits the county just before it crosses Horse Creek. On the USGS map there are no stage stations marked, the map just shows a road crossing the southern edge of Lincoln County.

The Goodnight Cattle Train is easier to follow because if follows Horse Creek. Entering from the south, Horse Creek parallels SH 71 for a distance. Just before the mesa, Horse Creek turns west Climbing up the hill. It soon turns into a small stream with groves of trees lining the stream bed. It Crosses SH 94 west of Punkin Center and in the spring the prairie is ablaze with the red and yellow blooms of the cacti. It is a small valley the creek has curved out, cool and inviting shade of the trees in the summer heat.

The Goodnight Cattle Trail is sprinkled with numerous communities/Post Offices along the route as it climbs up Horse Creek. Many an enterprising entrepreneur would set up a tent trading post or saloon along the trail. Here, miscellaneous supplies could be acquired by the drovers as they pushed their cattle west. Many of these communities were ranch houses where the mail could be picked up or sent.

There are not many roads in the area to follow the trail as it marches on to the gold fields. Yet it is an inviting stream on the vast plains. There are a few ranches in the area and a variety of communities are nearby. With a good map, one can meander the country roads and cross Horse Creek and follow for a bit then wind on to another road to cross back to Horse Creek again. No longer do the massive herds trot across the prairie. Today it is pastoral ranchland, dotted with grazing cattle, picturesque ranch homes nestled in the trees and a rolling land..

Hall Station
Sanborn, Kutch
And
Pierces

Driving along State Highway 94 one passes a highway sign for Hall Station. One looks and sees not much of anything. Here at the junction with County Road 11 is where Hall Station used to be. There is no mention of any kind of town being here but by lore/myth, a gentleman by the name of Hall operated a gas station on the SE corner of the junction. There are a few who say they still see old man Hall walking around his station. Late at night there have been reports of lights in the vacant field on the corner. Makes for some good tales on a full moon night.

On Lincoln County Assessor maps from the 1940's, Hall Station is shown as a community/school district. On the south end of this vacant lot are some relics and rubble piles. Here, there may have been a school house. There were numerous small districts that covered 20 to 50 square miles. A township was 35 square miles but that didn't always work.

To the south is Sanborn, at the corner of CR 11 and CR X is where the map shows the Post Office being located. The Sanborn sheep ranch was the Post Office in 1878. To the west of this intersection is where the USGS map shows another location for Sanborn. Going west on CR X one passes an old ranch location. Here may have been the Sanborn sheep ranch.

Figure 44 Alongside the road are corrals, chutes and abandoned buildings, marking where the sheep had been.

Sheep ranch conjures up Hollywood conflict between cow punchers and sheep men. Nearby is Horse Creek and along this route was the Goodnight Cattle Trail. Talking with a few old timers there are some stories of these two groups mixing like oil and water. There were the conflicts and the separation between the two groups. Sheep ranching was a major business across the eastern plains and there are the myths to go with the early days of ranching on the high plains. Today the sheep have all but disappeared and it is cattle that now graze on the prairie among the fields.

The Post Office at Sanborn lasted until Ira Kutch got the contract for the Post Office, in 1899. Kutch had its beginnings in a dugout on the banks of Horse Creek on the Lincoln and Elbert County line. The post Office lasted in the dugout until 1905 when it was moved again. Ira Kutch moved his Post Office north on CR 11 a few miles. Here a small community sprung up. Gas station, store, Blacksmith, dance hall, Baseball filed and dance barn plus some neighbors. Here the Post Office lasted till 1971.

Go north from Hall Station on CR 11 to CR 2A, turn west up the hill. At the crest of the hill one can look back at the far bank of Horse Creek to the NE. In the ranchers pasture there is a small depression and a rubble pile where the dugout used to be. Below the ridge cattle graze, a stream trickles along through the trees and some homes are tucked in the groves of trees in the stream bottom.

Going further west on CR 2A one comes to the Pierces. On the USGS map it is listed as being near here. Somewhere in the vicinity of CR 2A junction with CR 5 was the Pierces. Not sure if it was a store or what. Pierces would of been on the Goodnight cattle trail and the possibility of a trading post is possible or just may have been a ranch. There is a large home in the area reaching towards the clouds, looks like a small castle but it is on the wrong side of the road. On the other side is a stand of trees and ruts leading towards the creek. Who knows but it is fun to speculate. Sit there and imagine what it would have been like over 100 years ago driving cattle up the stream, headed for the goldfields. Ghost riders in the sky echoes over the prairie, hooves plodding over the ground, whistling bouncing among the tree branches and cookie is up ahead got the chow a goin.

Out over the vast prairie of southwestern Lincoln County numerous ghosts of days past, frolic or idle their time away. On SH 94, travelers whiz by.

McColin

Situated along the Goodnight Cattle Trail was the post Office of McColin. It is shown for two locations, one near the junction of CR W and 14, the other near CR V and CR 14. Traveling east on CR X from CR 11, the road zigs and zags a lot. CR V drops down into the Valley of Horse Creek. From the ridge one can look out across the expanse of the bottom land. On the far side of the creek is where the cattle traveled the Goodnight Cattle Trail.

Horse Creek makes a sharp bend here and on the far bend in a stand of trees. This would be the approximate location of McColin. The cattle trail would have passed this small outpost that more than likely was a ranch house. Let the gaze wander off to the south a couple of miles and this is where the other location for McColin would have been.

Today there are ranch homes along the course of Horse Creek. Some set back in the trees lining the creek, others up next to the road way. The road climbs a short hill then turns east again to follow along the creek, then east again to cross the creek. Here the creek goes underground and becomes a barren empty basin.

On a quiet day, one can pause, listen to the cattle as they trod up the trail to the gold camps. Yet this area had numerous sheep ranches. What kind of conflict was there? Were there gun fights between the herders and drovers? Are there graves that mark the conflicts along the trail?

Many of these early ranch workers were orphans and if they met their demise on the trail, there was no one to take care of them. Among the cemeteries in the area, none are noted as being a boot hill place, most are family plots, near communities and country churches. Often it was a shallow grave near where the incident happened. The combatants involved would fetch shovels. Then the drovers would move on and the herders back to their ranches. Records of these incidents were seldom recorded except in lore and tall tales.

Out across the prairies one can hear stories of lone riders trotting across the land. Occasionally bones are unearthed and stores unfold of what happened. Looking over the valley, what could have happened? What story awaits the traveler today?

Girard

Somewhere over yonder is where the community of Girard used to be. It fits the classic view of most people, situated on a flat plateau of the eastern Colorado plains, with nothing to view but the horizon. Girard is in the middle of somewhere, close to nowhere. The USGS map shows it being at the junction of CR 11 and CR S. There is a fence along the roadway and over there a ways is a ranch house, otherwise the intersection is empty. Down the road a piece is a stand of trees and some concrete chunks from a footer.

Figure 45 A ranch house is nestled in the hillside, with numerous springs near by.

Girard is one of those quiet places. One can hear the clouds float by, the chirping birds, fluttering wings and the scampering of the occasional critter. Look out across the prairie and the eye has no limit, the horizon reaches to eternity. Infinity takes on a whole new meaning, here the land is so empty, even the ghosts

would have no place to pause and ponder but to sit among the pasture grasses.

Yet, drive off to the horizon and the road drops off into one of the many creek valleys that dot the land. Over the land the buffalo roamed, followed by the Indians. Remains of these days can be found here and there. Many of the locals are excellent hunters of arrowheads and other artifacts left behind from centuries ago.

For the soul that ventures forth seeking out this lost community, do not be dis-heartened at seeing nothing. For the pioneer that settled here, saw opportunity, a place to call their own

Kendrick

South of SH 94, along the El Paso/Lincoln County line, about 6 miles is the community of Kendrick. The community church and few homes are all that's left of this rural community. The church is located at the junction of CR K and CR 3. Here there are some reminders of when more people lived in the area.

There is a stem wall still standing from a barn or shed, a well house, windmills and foundations. The church is a good sized compound of the church, pole building, parsonage and other sheds.

Nestled under some tall trees on the NW corner the church still is open and appears to be thriving. Dog guards the front yard of the parsonage and the grounds are well maintained. Across the road is a forlorn mail box collecting rust, the tree providing nice shade for the mail carrier that passes by. A small drive thru next to the tree, few weeds sprouting in the path among the grasses. The Kendrick Post Office closed years ago and now the mail comes from a neighboring town.

Near by are numerous farms and some memories of the "Dirty 30's. Abandoned homesteads sit next to the roadway, roofs gone, sheds falling over, piles of rubble and drifts of blow dirt in the windbreaks.

The lament of the settler can be heard in the whistling breezes of time. Flying along the ground the wind lifts the dust, swirling it over the land. The groans skid across the dirt, grasses bend to be buried, sand builds in the stock tank and the land thirsts for moisture.

Here one can see the ghosts of hope, the ghost of destruction and the ghost of renewal and determination. Many a family left their dreams in the 30's, others tenaciously hung on till the 50's when the next drought rolled out of the sky. Life ebbs and flows with the weather. The land nourishes the soul or drains the life out.

Many a ghost line the road, lamenting the good times, wailing at the harshness. Across the field it walks, looking for hope, determination etched on the countenance.

Kendrick is a classic look at life of the pioneer, their struggles and the triumphs. The song of the prairie echoes over the trees, bounding on the plain.

Cowan's

Cowan's, the community Post Office on wheels, the USGS map shows five different locations for the Post Office. As it moved from ranch house to ranch house, it appears to of kept the name Cowan's. On the county map it shows a Cowan's school district in the area.

The Cowan's community covered a vast area, there was the school house, couple of cemeteries and a church in the area. Here one can take the dusty back country roads and get a peek at life more than 100 years ago. The roads climb hills, showing hope, revealing sorrow. Crossing a ridge, angling across a pasture the road passes small sand dunes, reminders of drier years, when the wind would rearrange the dust and leave it in stacks. Riding up over a hill, hope springs forth, lush green grasses slice across the horizon. Springs dot the creek banks, small pools of water glisten in the sun, deer stand in belly deep grass.

The lifeline of the prairie ushers from the ground, nourishing the grasses, wildlife, and trees climb towards the clouds the birds chirp contently in this oasis. A small stream headwaters in the area, giving life to a dry parched land. Here CR 10 ends crossing this slash of green. The road winds through the front yards going up to the other side to CR D following the other side of the creek bank. There are other houses nearby looking out over the waving green grasses.

The map shows there being a Post Office at this junction of CR 10 and CR D. One can see why it would be a great place to settle. Traveling on west on CR D to CR 8 junction is to the next location of a Cowan Post Office. Here at the junction of two county roads are a few cattle grazing in the pasture. Going on west on CR D, one leaves the green little valley behind. It is now mostly rolling gentle lands with a view to the west of Pikes Peak. There are some ranch houses along the route. When CR D ends at CR 4 is where the map showed another location for Cowan. Here there is a rubble pile and some foundations.

Figure 46 Trees and buildings where the road crosses an old location for Cowans.

This may have been a Post Office/General Store combination. Today it is surrounded by pasture and empty land. The harsh reality of the Dust Bowl can be seen as eyes travel the horizon. Sparse grasslands have been scooped out by windy blasts, dust and sand deposited in small dunes. Dreams of many settlers were dashed by the dirt storms, leaving behind abandoned homes.

Figure 47 A pile of rubble is all the remains.

Making a big loop, one can angle north to CR M, east to CR 5, north to CR J and then west back to the Cowan's schoolhouse. On the SW corner of CR J and CR 10 is the tattered and weathered schoolhouse. Here the families entrusted their children's learning to a school teacher they hired. It was also a community building for meetings and special events, and it was the polling place for elections.

Toady it sits empty, listening to the winds of time travel through the rafters. The rest house out back still stands, looking out across the pasture of other days. Time has traveled on and the ghosts silently sit on the tufts of prairie grasses. The sounds of squealing children silent, no clanging of a school bell, here was an era many knew not.

Across the road from the school building is some rubble piles, footers and a well house. Many of these communities would provide housing for the teacher and this lot may have housed the teacher. Stand on the hill ridge, watch the clouds float by, listen to the silence, the echoes do not return.

One has made a full circle around the Cowan community..... almost. To the east on CR J is a substation and pumping station for a gas line. Here is where another Cowan Post Office was shown to be. The station is named Cowan's substation, underneath gas flows where a community Post Office once was housed. Other side of the road is some old corrals and footers from some buildings that once stood in the area.

Look off to the east, down in the draw is some trees, here in Dead Horse Creek is where another Cowan's Post Office was shown. To east where CR 12 would have been is the cemetery. It is marked by a gate and there are a few headstones still there. The wooden crosses have long been gone.

Cowan gives a classic look back into a time that has long disappeared. The schoolhouse, mail rooms, stores, churches and graveyards. Families lived out their dreams, many met sorrow, others tenaciously hung on. Ghosts sitting alongside the roads, have many stories to tell, so often they are not heard.

CR J goes west from SH 71 and makes a dog leg south a bit then continues. Passing replaced creek bridges. Up over a ridge to CR 13 and one is in Dead Horse Creek. The road had made a curve to cross the creek but the county has straightened out the curve at Cowan with a culvert. Here is the grave yard just before the creek. A bit further on is the stand of trees where a ranch house once stood.

Forder

Forder was a sheep ranch in the late 1800's. In 1901 it was awarded a Post Office. The location was at the intersection of SH 71 and CR R in the southern end of Lincoln County. The government map shows 3 Post Office locations for Forder. In 1920 the Post Office was moved, SH 71 and CR J. Two years later it was moved again, a short distance north to SH 71 and CR M.

The Forder sheep ranch was located along Horse Creek that parallels SH 71. Today Forder Ranch raises cattle and is still on the banks of Horse Creek. Situated among the trees lining the creek, it is set back from the highway.

Being a sheep ranch, one could see the potential for conflict between the cattle men driving herds along Horse Creek and the sheep men. County maps show a cemetery near the location of the 1920 Forder. It is in a pasture off the road a distance. So, if it is a family plot or something else is a mystery. Yet there were probably violent clashes between the different factions.

Dropping down the plateau into Horse Creek basin one can catch a glimpse of life changing. In the creek basin the land changes. The prairie grasses become sparse because there is less rainfall. The creek provides water for the cattle but very little grass to graze. Dust ghosts float over the land during dry years, cattle cling to the shade of the creek trees, life paces different in the drier land.

Traveling on highway 71, there is nothing to see. The land has become empty of any structures that may have marked where the Post Office was. There are ranch houses that set off the highway back in among the trees and cattle dot the grass land. Abandoned building sit on a corner, reminder of other days gone past. The occasional ghost can be spotted at times meandering over the land in search of............ Here the land hasn't varied much.

Figure 48 The moon rises as a thunderhead builds over the eastern plains.

Hollywood

The headlights bounced off the weeds, casting waving shadows as the pickup rolled down the dirt road to the town dump. The moon was playing peek a boo with the clouds as they rushed over head. As the moon darted out from behind the clouds, shadows would dance across the beam of the headlamps of the pickup creating an eerie evening. Suddenly Gary shouted out, "Stop, look at that?"

Steve pushed the clutch in and the pickup rolled to a stop. Gary was all excited, bouncing up and down, rolling the window down to get a better look. "Come on, turn the pickup to shine the lights on it," Gary shouted. Excitement and fear filled the pickup. Steve slid the pickup into reverse, cranked the wheel and lights traveled across the field.

About 100 yards away in the field a lantern bounced along, heading for the grove of trees. Steve whispers to Gary, "What is that? I see the lantern but nothing else." Awe struck the pair sat there, eyes bugged out wide, jaw slack. Steve kept moving the pickup backwards keeping the lantern in his headlights.

Across the field the lantern flowed. Nothing appeared to be carrying it, suspend in the air. Soon the lantern reached the stand of trees and disappeared.

The two boys were quiet for some time. They had heard stories of the ghosts that lived in an area called Hollywood. They had driven down to the town dump before to hunt rats and have a couple of beers. This is the first time they had seen the lantern moving across the land.

Steve got the pickup turned around and back over the railroad tracks they bounced, headed back to town.

Figure 49 A bit of the wall and piles of rubble mark where the railroad had shops and the roundhouse.

Next day at school they were talking to some friends about what they had seen. Friends looked in disbelief, a few asked how many drinks they had drank. Soon an older boy sauntered up to the group and heard what was being said. He piped up and asked them, "Did you see the bluish lights also?" "They float over the field at times, maybe 10-12 feet up." The group stood silent for a moment, for here was somebody that confirmed what their friends had said.

Hollywood, stirs up lots of stories among a few locals in Limon. For years there have been stories like this and most people have attributed them to the hobos and bums that hang out in the area. The Rock Island had built a roundhouse and other buildings in the area at the end of the 1800's. For years this was the life of the town and the tramps had been riding the rails through here for years. Nearby is the Big Sandy Creek, with overpasses and creek banks, making good protection for the hobos.

So to say the strange happening in the area belong to the passing by hobos is not a stretch. One can walk in the area today and see where they have been, read their signs for what is available in Limon for hand outs.

Yet one asks, what is causing the lights, why is there no one with the lantern? The ghostly aura of Hollywood persists. Walk along the tracks, look in among the ruins of the roundhouse, there are times it is like someone is watching them.

Is it an old railroad worker walking across the field to check on his shop? Where do the floating bluish lights come from?

A ways west along the abandoned railroad tracks sits a small house, may have been a section house at one time.

Mom and her son are sitting in the living room when they hear the door squeak as it opens. Mom and son look at each other. Mom says, no it can't be, I bolted the door from the inside. Footsteps cross the floor, they rush to the front door and see nothing. The bolt is in place, locked from the inside. Sometime later mom is at home and hears the door opening. Looking through the doorway, she sees nothing but hears footsteps on the floor. That evening she is talking with the neighbor. Neighbor says to her, "You have someone living in your attic." "Quite often I'll see her standing looking out the window, down towards the where the railroad tracks used to be."

Mom is all wide eyed but it dawns on her why the door opens and she hears someone walking in the house. Short while later, mom finds another house and they move.

The Spirits of Clifford

Below the horizon the sun settled, the cool of the evening was moving over the land. It had been a long hot summer day and the shade of the porch was inviting. Chairs were placed on the floor, shadows reclined and matches were struck. It was an evening ritual, sit on the porch, have a smoke and converse about the day. Cigarette embers glowed, voices traveled over the way, the whistle of the night train could be heard in the distance.

Soon the old time puffer would pause at the station, unload some packages, maybe a passenger and pick one up. Soon the chuffs of the engine would echo out across the valley as it began to build up steam to roll on down the tracks. It would be clear of town and one could look across the rails to the Montgomery Ward house and see them still sitting on the front porch, glowing cigarettes and voices engaged with each other.

Those days have long since passed but the old Montgomery Ward house still stands today. Well weathered and neglected. The porch roofs have collapsed, windows are open and one can see the lights of the roof dance across the panes.

Here resides a classic haunted house. On a warm evening one can gaze across the tracks and watch the shadows dance around the old house, hear the sounds of days past reverberate over the fields.

Clifford is the home of numerous spirits. To know these spirits one should travel back before the white man trod over the land.

Coon Creek is just to the east of the old Ghost Town of Clifford and on its banks the Indians built a sweat lodge. Here the Indians could sit and commune with their creator. Build a fire in the rock pit, heat the rocks up and pour water over them. In a covered lodge the Indians would cleanse themselves, chanting and singing, sweat rolling off their bodies. As the heat sweltered, out the lodge they would leap, jumping into the pools of Coon Creek. Splashing around the Indians would cool off and finish the cleansing ritual. Here their spirits were, here the Indians could sing to their creator.

Figure 50 Graves sit next to the roadway.

For decades the Indians were not bothered, then in the early 1800's, the United States bought the Louisiana Purchase and sent explorers out into their new territory. With reports about the land reaching back east, there were more travelers going west seeking riches. Then gold was discovered. The beginning of the conflict with the Indians began. Right through the spiritual place went the Smoky Hill Trail, soon to be followed by stagecoaches and freighters.

With the springs of Coon Creek and the ponds of water, the early traveler stopped here. The stage station was called Mirage and it was on the banks of Coon Creek, near the Indian sweat lodge site. Not liking this, the Indians launched numerous attacks on the stage station and attacked many of the early gold seekers traveling the route. Later the railroad showed up and the conflict with the Indians escalated. There were more attacks by the Indians and more people were killed. Soon the calvary was called and the Indians fled and there was some peace, except for the spirits that were left behind. In to the 1900's, there were reports of Indians wandering through the area, pausing along the banks of Coon Creek. Today one has to look closely, but what are the shadows wandering through the woods? Such begins the stories of ghosts walking the land.

Clifford became a station stop for the railroad, stores were built, a schoolhouse and homes. Today the only reminders that Clifford existed are the various concrete footers along the tracks and depressions for cellars. Clifford is fodder for all types of stories. The old haunted house across the tracks, on private property, is but one story. The Indian Spirits is another. There are the graves, next to the road, of the family and young children and there is the buried treasure.

There are stories that some robbers buried their ill gotten loot in a gully just east of Clifford. Supposedly they used some dutch ovens to bury the gold coins in and then marked the sites with marked rocks. Over the years, rocks with markings have cropped up, sending a treasure hunting frenzy off into the gullies to the east. But if one looks closely at the banks along the gulch, they can see the laughing faces of the robbers, sitting next to the buried gold coins. Even today, locals swear that the treasure is still out there.

Next to the road are six gravesites, not much is known about them. Yet during the era of their deaths, there were numerous epidemics that roared across the plains. Entire families would be wiped out by these plagues sweeping the land. It is said, one can be still near the graves and hear the low sobbing of a mother for her children. Today cars pass by not even noticing the tiny cemetery.

A Ghost Town full of spirits and stories yet to be told, off the main highway a short distance, bypassed by time and people.

Can the spirits of the Indians still be felt, the pools of Coon Creek still flow. The schoolhouse still stands, out back is the shed for coal, can the school marm be seen hustling out there on a cold morning to fire the stove up. Are the drummer boys still sitting on the porch of the old house having a cigarette. Will the ghost riders of the stage come charging into the station for a mule change. Then there is the ghost train as it puffs along the rails, whistle echoing along the valley. The robbers are they still sitting along the gully banks. Indians come racing into view, arrows flying, settlers scattering, the Calvary charging out of the woods. The Wild West is but a toss of the imagination away.

Haunted Farms

Genoa

A few miles north of Genoa, CO is the old haunted house, well it used to be. Now it is marked by a few trees, some years ago it was torn down and only a few memories float over the ground. Here the local school kids had decorated the old abandoned homestead for a number of years. The youthful fertile imagination abounded of many tall tales of ghosts roaming the place.

There were stories of figures standing in the windows watching passing cars. The house was built of white block and the shadows of the moon would dance over the house. Shadows would flit and hover in the trees out back. There were spooks that lived in the abandoned farm house and the school kids built the legend larger each year it was decorated.

There is an abandoned farm to the southeast of the haunted house that has stories of ghosts and mysterious lights. Here many a scary story was heard in the halls of the schoolhouse. There would be times a girl would blanche out from having been there, a boy would have a blank stare looking into nothing.

One has to go back to 1911 to understand the stories of that place. In 1911 it was homesteaded. The young settler had traveled to the area in 1910 and found his place to homestead. He returned back east, married his sweetheart and they set out for the new town of Genoa to begin their life. Here was his dream, a small creek with a spring on it, gentle rolling land around it for farming and the creek bottom for his cattle.

A house was built, land was plowed and out buildings were put up. Children were born and the farm was prospering. Life was good for the settler, he had a wife, children and a place to call his own. Nearby was a school for his children, he had helped to build. His oldest boy would lead his younger brother and sister to school and they would come home at night and do their chores. Then in the 1920's, influenza struck the plains. First it struck down his middle boy, then his daughter, oldest boy and wife all died within weeks of each other. The settler dug graves for his family on the bluff overlooking the creek. With his family gone, he left the land and disappeared. No one knows where he went, yet on the bluff were the small markers of the graves.

Another farmer bought the land at an auction and that is

when the stories began. He was working the land when heard the squeal of children playing. Looking on the bluff he saw shadows bounding through the grass. The farmer let it pass and said nothing for that was only time he had heard or seen anything. He said to himself, "It is just my imagination."

Some years later his son had found it was a good place to bring his girl friend to and park. He could drive along the creek bottom on a shelf below the rise and it was protected and out of sight from the road. A few trees had grown up and it was a quiet place to park.

Fall was approaching and they had been to the barn dance down the road. The boy and girl were giggling as they bounced over the road. Turning off into his father's place and rolling down the embankment to the trees they went. He had some cigarettes and some shine and they were going to enjoy it before going on home. Suddenly the girl shrieked, hair was standing on end, fingers were pointing across the creek to the bluff. The boys jaw dropped. A large figure stood on the bluff, hands in the air and crying. A lament that pierced the soul, traveled up the spine and bent a strong heart.

There by the graves the figure floated, wailing into the night, screeching echoes floating over the land. The car jumped to life, wheels spinning, up the hill they fled, wanting to get away from this place. Next week at school, one should of heard the stories. Like wildfire the lore spread growing larger with each telling. Soon there were other kids going out there at night, parking and watching, nothing. The boy and girl soon became a butt of jokes.

With the story and seeing the place the farm became a popular place for the local kids to party. Being protected and out of sight they could party away and make jokes about the ghosts.

Couples of years later the local kids were out at the farm for a Saturday night party. There was the liquor, music and boisterous bragging conversations. With the full moon and a calm night is was a pleasant night to be out. With midnight approaching a wail shattered the reverie of the kids. Hair was climbing over their skin, stomachs were dropping, hearts were pounding as the wail rolled over the bottom slicing the moonlight.

There on the far bluff was a large white figure, floating over the graves, tears rolling, voice raised to a wail.

Motors roared to life, kids were piling into cars, wheels screeching up the hill. Other kids stood there frozen, time had stopped, jaws were gasping. Never before had they seen or heard anything like it. School the next week was abuzz and more curios people ventured out to the farm.

Today the farm is much like the schoolhouse, a vacant lot marked by an old fence.

55088699R00097

Made in the USA
Charleston, SC
20 April 2016